MOVIES 1927 TO 1941

Books by Pare Lorentz

CENSORED: THE PRIVATE LIFE OF THE MOVIES
(with Morris L. Ernst)

THE ROOSEVELT YEAR: 1933

THE RIVER

MOVIES 1927 TO 1941

LORENTZ ON FILM

PARE LORENTZ

HOPKINSON AND BLAKE, PUBLISHERS
NEW YORK

This compilation is dedicated to my first
and last magazine editors, Norman Anthony
of Judge and Otis L. Wiese of McCall's, for
remembrances of cordial times past, and
because more than once they risked their
own security by refusing to allow their
business offices to have me either censored
or fired.

Pare Lorentz

Contents

THE EARLY FORTIES

Prologue

by KING VIDOR

I FIRST met Pare Lorentz in 1929 on a cold afternoon in New York
City just after he had viewed one of my films, the first all-Negro
motion picture, *Hallelujah*. His interest in every detail of the picture—how certain scenes were staged, how some of the performers
were cast, where we found the "locations"—made me realize that
here was a sincere student of filmmaking expressing his love for
films by writing about them.

By midnight of that same evening, I had come to realize that his
questioning went far beyond my film. I was being cross-examined
about everything I had learned about filmmaking. I suppose this
accounts for the durable friendship that has existed between us.

He was an able interpreter of the films of a glorious era. Well
before the advent of sound synchronization, he likened film form to
musical form. In reviewing *Sunrise*, he saw Murnau's structure as
a symphony. He set forth the *auteur* theory in filmmaking, seeing
the necessity of a film expressing the individuality of one man.

Unlike some contemporary critics of films, Lorentz tried to be
constructive on one hand while taking the picture apart with the
other. He loved movies too much to wallow in the negative smog
that has characterized some of our most popular reviewers.

He says of the first film version of Theodore Dreiser's *An American Tragedy*, "It is an important picture which Josef von Stern-

1

berg has turned out, and not because of the novel but in spite of it."

He showed perception in spotting unusual ability well in advance of the general discovery. In reviewing *The 39 Steps*, he made note of the peculiar talent of the "chubby Cockney" who directed it, Alfred Hitchcock.

In his review of *Gone With The Wind*, he analyzes it purely as a stupendous movie, wisely making no comparisons with the book. In fact, it can readily be surmised that he had not read the book. A book is a book and a movie is a movie, but so many reviewers try to show their erudition by making useless comparisons between the two.

When someone assumes the position of a critic, he automatically takes on the responsibility of evaluating not merely for himself. He must also have the ability of communicating this evaluation to his readers. This necessitates an ability to penetrate into the motives and purposes of those who contributed to or guided the various elements that characterized the completed product. The critic should be able to differentiate between the story, the adaptation, the direction, the acting, the editing. He must say more than "I liked it" or "I didn't like it." He must be thoroughly capable of analyzing why it is a good film or a bad one. This ability comes through in all of Lorentz's reviews.

It is one of the idiosyncrasies of the annual Academy Awards that a film can win the best picture award and yet the man who made it sometimes is never even mentioned in the voting.

While going to see hundreds of films each year and reporting on them, Lorentz still found time to speak out as a prophet and commentator of the new art in general.

Long before the Supreme Court granted equal freedom of expression to the filmmakers he wrote: "Censorship militates in favor of emasculated uniformity. Always troubled by the censors, the movies are now in that state of maidenly apprehension so typical of all corporations in the United States."

Long before chains of moderate-sized art theatres sprang up throughout America and provided a reasonable outlet for a Fellini, a Bergman or an Antonioni film, he wrote, "So long as movie companies make pictures aimed at the common denominator of the mass audiences required in the cathedrals of the motion pictures, we shall have celluloid drivel imposed upon us."

Pare Lorentz to me was one of the first who firmly believed that motion picture film was the strongest medium of expression. When I went to England in 1938 to film *The Citadel*, I persuaded him to drop what he was doing and come along with me so that I could be stimulated by a running discussion of what filmmaking was all about, particularly as it related to the subject at hand. We went by ship to provide plenty of time for yakking, and if I ever lacked enthusiasm or inspiration these talks with Lorentz revived them in me.

Pare Lorentz's love and appreciation for films burst forth in all honesty when he made *The Plow That Broke The Plains* as a project for the United States Department of Agriculture, a documentary film that recounts with a harmonious blend of poetic images, narrative, and music the agricultural misuse of the Great Plains that resulted in the Dust Bowl of the 1930s. With this first film, he formulated a unique and individual style in the documentary form.

This personal approach was verified and amplified by *The River* (1937), the history of the Mississippi River Basin and the effect of the Tennessee Valley Authority on the area. In this movie he further demonstrated the potential of the documentary film as a powerful medium. Both in the United States and in England, where the two films were commercially and artistically successful, wide spread discussion resulted, not only of the problems presented but also of his original documentary approach to filmmaking.

As a result of the success of these two government movies, in the summer of 1938 President Franklin D. Roosevelt established the United States Film Service and appointed Lorentz as its Chief.

This is a book by Pare Lorentz, the film critic, but if you read between the lines, there is much to be learned about Lorentz, the cinema prophet, and Lorentz, the filmmaker.

January, 1975

The Late Twenties

SUNRISE

To CALL a motion picture reviewer a critic, in the strict sense of the word, is as misnomial as calling a Chicago hog butcher a surgeon. "One who judges of the qualities of anything by some standard" implies precedent by which to judge. So far, most of the movies that have been made since Edison invented the moving picture have been a mongrel, illegitimate breed, a mechanical curiosity, with the less said about them the better. Regardless of the wealth of the motion picture industry, regardless of the host of writers and playwrights who litter the Pacific Coast, there are but two or three men who have felt the real possibilities of the motion picture as a medium for expressing human emotions with photography and musical accompaniment. Therefore, there is no real precedent by which to judge the motion picture. There have been a barren dozen made in the manner in which a motion picture should be made.

Fred W. Murnau, who directed *The Last Laugh* and whose latest film is *Sunrise*, is one of the men who has grasped the great possibilities of his craft.

Sunrise is conceived and written like a symphony. In fact, Murnau sub-titles his picture "A Song of Two Humans." The accompanying music is synchronized so that the entire motion picture is an audible and visual symphony, carefully divided into three movements.

The motion picture opens on the gray shores of a small fishing village. You see a man of the soil seduced by a woman from the city. With no more introduction than that, the story begins. You see the bewildered peasant marching across the misty moors to meet his lecherous paramour, while his quiet wife is dumb and miserable at the incomprehensible curse that has poisoned their love. The woman from the city has sunk her teeth into the jugular vein of this man; she is taking his life blood and destroying a household. In the dark rushes, she inflames him with prophecies of life in the city and dances a mad, macabre dance of passion in the shadow of the black cliffs, and then plants the idea of murder in the man's seething brain.

That is the story—the attempted murder and the peace after the storm. It is all done with the careful hand of a man who has a fine feeling, a great understanding of humanity. You get the smell of the salt air, the stink of the marsh; you see the pitiful figure of a man moved to inevitable tragedy by stark passion, driven mad by the pounding of his blood. It has the hard, granite strength of O'Neill's "Beyond the Horizon."

But understand that this feeling, this atmosphere, is not created by second-hand dramaturgy. It is portrayed by a series of direct pictures that seem beautiful enough to have been struck off by one of the old Flemish masters, accompanied by music that ebbs and flows with the rhythm of the story.

Then something happens. It is as shocking as though "Beyond the Horizon," in the second act, should produce a musical comedy ballet; as incongruous as John D. Rockefeller suddenly appearing in a grass skirt before a Standard Oil directors' meeting and doing the hootchie-kootchie dance. *Sunrise* deliberately becomes slapstick and at loose ends, and my theory is that William Fox either would not let Murnau produce the film as he wanted or else scared him so that he felt an American audience would not stand for a movie without a Prohibition joke in it. It is as terrible as Hamlet suddenly leaving off his soliloquy to do the Black Bottom.

Even so, you will find *Sunrise* one of the most stimulating pictures in the city. You will understand the power this man Murnau has with his craft. You will see a motion picture that, until the second, or slapstick movement, uses no cast-off turns from the theatre but that surges ahead with powerful fundamental strokes in a sure and original manner.

It is too bad *Sunrise* has to include an apology. It just missed being a great picture. It is still a great picture in comparison with the other screen showings on Broadway, but its weakness should be a lasting mortification for Murnau.

Judge, October 15, 1927

RUNNING WILD

IT'S A shame the way they treat W. C. Fields. His last three pictures have been based on this formula: the poverty-stricken, henpecked clerk suddenly acquires wealth, subdues his family, and becomes boss of the ranch. Now Fields is a good juggler, a good actor, and a great comedian, and he deserves better treatment. There is one scene in *Running Wild* in which he goes in to ask for a raise and gives one of the finest and most poignant characterizations I have ever seen on the screen. Before this, when he rehearses his speech and goes through that pantomime, you see Fields at his best—the showman with the grand gestures, the gold watch chain and the black cigar. And while the scenario itself is about as original as a Bruce Barton piece, as clever as a Coolidge speech of welcome, and as mirth-provoking as a pernicious case of spinal meningitis, *Running Wild* is still worth seeing because Fields is in it.

Judge, July 9, 1927

THE UNKNOWN

TODD BROWNING is a good and a courageous movie director. First in *The Mystic,* then in *Unholy Three* and now with *The Unknown,* Browning has consistently tried to develop the most difficult of all movie effects: the sinister and supernatural. Consider the task. Even the worst moron has seen so many climaxes in the movies that he now feels confident that the hero will come to the rescue in time and has little tendency to become alarmed by any situation. Again, the inanimate cinema does not allow the emotional reaction that the sibilant whisperings and sudden silences of the stage can create. The supernatural effect in the movie must be built up by photography and pantomime. Yet Browning understands his medium so well that he has achieved his effect, with varying degrees of success, in his three movies.

Instead of depending on ham writers, Browning builds up his own scenarios to fit his material, as a good football coach develops his plays around his players. He has utilized Lon Chaney's ability as a contortionist again in *The Unknown,* his latest picture.

It is not as good as *Unholy Three.* Chaney plays the role of an armless member of a gypsy circus troop, and while Browning has tried to create a gruesome situation, the spectacle of Chaney eating with his toes is no more gruesome than a quick lunch addict eating peas with a knife. The picture also has too many sub-titles. Still, it's much better than the ordinary movie.

Judge, July 9, 1927

UNDERWORLD

Underworld was really interesting and entertaining because it moved fast, because it had some remarkable photography, and because the acting was convincing. The story, written by Ben

Hecht, is based on an actual incident of gang warfare in Chicago, and deals with the exploits of a modern gangster in that city. However, while the story has a few weak places, and the ending is very ordinary, the picture is tremendously effective. The use of machine guns seems real, and you get the feeling of the terrible violence that does exist in the gang alleys of our Chicago of today.

George Bancroft is an excellent and hard-working actor, and his acting, combined with the direction of Von Sternberg, makes *Underworld* a picture well worth seeing.

Judge, September 24, 1927

THE FIRST NIGHTERS

THE MOVIE first night has evolved into a Broadway institution. At one time, movies used to try to slink into town unobserved, but now that Carl Van Vechten, *et al.*, have discovered that the movie is a struggling Art the movie first night has become a manifestation quite analogous to John Roach Straton's current forecast of the Judgment Day.

The first night movie audience can be roughly classified into three groups: the Trade, the Friends, and the Press. The first group consists mainly of grubby little fellows in uncertain evening dress whom you will see bumping around the lobby looking like so many black and white pouter pigeons. Their conversation is entirely statistical and never under five figures.

The cousins and the sisters and the aunts of the movie producers really bring color and variety to the first night and make it worthwhile. They take their openings seriously. Papa may wear a Prince Albert, black trousers, and a colored shirt, neatly topped with an August half-price sale straw hat, and Mama may stick a tiara on top of the permanent that looks like Woolworth's Yuletide set of Christmas decorations. Still and all, they bring the right deference, the proper adulation that should attend a virgin offering of the great art. They block the aisles hours before the curtain rises and fold their arms and wait in humble complacency for a sight of a movie star or of Uncle Benny, who makes the stars.

You may confuse the typewriter maulers who make up the minority press group with the chaps who sell chewing gum and pencils in front of the theatres, but you can differentiate them easily because the chewing gum venders carry canes.

The box office has instructions to inform all passersby that the house is sold out, even though there may be enough seats in the balcony to comfortably lodge the entire Indiana delegation of United Elks. However, this stunt is not indigenous to movie first nights and is merely one of the Broadway encores the producers have added to their repertoire.

There is always a battery of photographers and cameramen to add to the furor of one of these movie melees. At the last one I attended, I was struggling in front of the theatre trying to extricate my left elbow from the ample fold of a neighboring shirt front when suddenly a squad of photographers marched down the street, set up their cameras and began to lay down a barrage of flashlight shots. Thinking that Will Hays or at least Douglas Fairbanks was doing a center rush into the theatre, I carelessly disregarded my elbow for the moment and tried to spot the arriving celebrity. However, after the fourteenth explosion I realized that they were taking pictures of me!

I dashed over and, quickly disguising my embarrassment and the loss of the left elbow joint, told one of the men that there was some mistake—that it was obviously a case of mistaken identity, and that I would be only too glad to help him locate the missing celebrity.

"I don't give a damn who you are," he came back dogmatically. "They hired us to come here and take flashlight pictures for an hour and we're gonna do it. Try this one without the hat."

The opening night of the Colony Theatre was attended by a brilliant crowd of notables in formal attire. Now under the direction of Hugo Riesenfeld, the opening program was original and entertaining and vastly pleasing to the brilliant first night audience. The picture, *The Cat and the Canary*, was adapted from the mystery play, and filled as it was with novel settings and camera effects, was very effective, although a bit tiresome. However, it met with the unanimous approval of the scintillating first nighters.

Judge, October 1, 1927

DON'TS

THE FEDERAL Trade Commission has been raising cain with the movie producers these last few months and the Paramount Company is now under indictment for violating the anti-trust law. The producers have flagrantly been operating against the law, most people agree, and the Commission seems to be on their track in earnest just now. The Hollywood fat boys called a conference to try to whitewash the industry's record and Will Hays gave way to a forensic orgasm in which he proclaimed that "the movie industry is the most highly competitive industry ever known to man, and there is absolutely no chance for the incompetent or the unfit to survive." So much for Will Hays.

The producers then got together and told the chairman of the Federal Commission that they would all be very good boys if he would only let them off this time. Not only that, but they laid down a code of ethics called "Resolutions and Don'ts," which was tearfully presented by Mr. Louis Mayer, the spokesman for the producers. This list comprised about thirty-five "Don'ts." I reprint a few of them here so that you may realize the import of this great regeneration that is sweeping through the Hollywood bagnios and making them as clean as Salvation Army missions. These are some of the things ruled out:

1. Pointed profanity either by title or lip. God, Lord, Jesus, and Christ are barred unless they are used reverently in connection with religious ceremonies. Also, hell, damn, gawd or any other profane or evil expression, however it may be spelled. (Explanatory note: you can't call a man a "so-and-so" and spell it "old beanbag" and expect to get away with it.)

2. Any licentious or suggestive nudity, in fact or in silhouette, or

any lecherous or licentious notice by any characters in the picture.

3. Any illegal traffic in drugs.

4. White slavery.

5. Miscegenation.

6. Sex hygiene.

7. Scenes of actual childbirth, or in silhouette.

8. Ridicule of the clergy.

9. Wilful offense to any nation, race, or creed. Be it further resolved that special care be exercised in the manner in which the following subjects are treated to the end that vulgarity and suggestiveness may be eliminated and that good taste may be exercised:

(a) The use of the flag.

(b) International relations. (Putting unfavorable light on another country's religion, history, institutions, prominent people or citizenry.)

As the producers have chosen to carry the cross of purity from the trade conference back to Hollywood, I feel that it is only fair for me, in my modest role as reviewer, to also undergo a moral housecleaning. I, therefore, have set up the following "Don'ts" as a moral code for the coming years. I promise I shall:

1. Never see a picture of, or a word on the screen, pertaining to Mother, without crying softly.

2. Never speak harshly to any usher, without first making sure that he is well and happy, and is enjoying his work.

3. Not throw rocks at old ladies, unless they have first demonstrated an unusual agility.

4. Never fall in love with a movie star, unless such nudity is vouched for as being entirely without suggestiveness or moral obligation, actually or in sihouette.

5. Never speak a word of impertinence to the editor. (Reservation note: not until after I get a raise, anyhow.)

6. Renew my membership in the Boy Scouts.

7. Never gamble again; that is, with any member of the Judge staff. (This includes Judge Junior.)

8. Never offend anybody who in any way is connected with anything in any way whatsoever.

9. Never read a line written by any movie reviewer. (Exceptions: John S. Cohen, Jr. and Robert Sherwood.)

10. Never see another motion picture the rest of my life.

Judge, November 12, 1927

THE CROWD

KING VIDOR proves that his superb direction of *The Big Parade* was no fortunate accident and turns out another magnificent work in *The Crowd*.

With restraint and delicacy that put to shame all the flutterings ever released by the Gish family, Eleanor Boardman gives a remarkably good performance as the wife of the boy-who-was-going-to-be-President, and a new-found star, James Murray, ably supports her. The story is consistent up until the conclusion, and the entire production is smoothed and polished into a beautiful symmetry by the crafty hand of Mr. Vidor.

The idea of the picture, explained by its title, lends itself happily to screen exploitation. It is a sympathetic and accurate study of a member of our modern army of clerks. The great regiments of insurance workers moving in time to the minute hand of the clock, the steel and granite robot warrens belching their squirming cargo into the narrow streets of the city, perspiring masses of flesh seeking relief under the white glare of lights at Coney—these are things to delight the imagination of a modern artist, and Vidor turns the cold eye of the camera on this barren spectacle with breathtaking results.

The story of *The Crowd* is simple and moving. The boy-who-was-going-to-be-President subscribes to a clerk's life, enters upon married life and lives in a two-room-and-bath apartment with a vigorous egotism that he is different, that he is going to be somebody. He escapes the reality of his futile existence with this delusion until the death of his child beats him into submission. The weak point of the story is presented here—down and out, he comes back with a glowing burst of courage that makes him a heroic figure, then, like a slap in the face, the director shows him once more caught up by the mob, laughing and giggling and crowing to the monotonous beat of the crowd's pulse.

His regeneration was too convincing and his family's character too sympathetic to dismiss so summarily their lives, but this inconsistent conclusion is not important enough to dull the brilliance of the picture.

Judge, March 10, 1928

BUSTER KEATON

SOME months ago I became so bewildered and sickened with the celluloid Hollywood menu that I collected all my dour theories in a neat knapsack and hiked to the office of Dr. A. A. Brill, one of the most learned as well as courteous psychologists in the country. I felt that the backbone of the nation was developing gangrene from the constant imposition of such rot as is concocted by the Messrs. Zukor and *confrères* and that no civilization could long remain sturdy with a majority of its inhabitants having their perceptions of life, love, hate, and immortality perpetually gassed by the lethal stench belching from the Golden Coast studios.

Dr. Brill denied everything. He said, in part, that no matter how lacking in artistic proportion, the movies did no harm to the morons who support them, and that one could take away from a movie only what he needed.

But if it happens that you are the father or mother of eighteen children, the sole support of an alcoholic grandfather, that you have a third mortgage on the home, and believe that woman is God's greatest work of art, then it is possible you may find some needed consolation in movies such as *Fifty-Fifty Girl*.

Of course, it is not all grief. There is Buster Keaton, for instance, and his picture *Steamboat Bill, Jr.*, which made the week livable. Of course, if one were to live up to the title of critic it would be possible to say "Well, here's another bum comedy, full of slapstick falls, with a sappy love story, and a big opportunity all shot—the whole Mississippi to work with, including a complete set of Mark Twain stories, and all you get is a couple of good sequences." But I still have a spark of gratitude left, and after seeing Mr. Lasky's *Fifty-Fifty Girl* I felt like sending Mr. Keaton a fan note thanking him for a few minutes of real enjoyment.

I enjoy Keaton's pictures thoroughly, and while his latest production does include such old favorites as a tornado which blows houses and trees on the frozen head of our hero and a wide-eyed heroine who peers into the camera with the angelic expression of a child anticipating a great big stocking full of goodies from Santa Claus, it has several bits of pantomime between Ernest Torrence and Buster Keaton which are sheer amusement. You may be bored at the long intervals during which the blank-faced hero slides across the Mississippi delta on one ear, but just wait for the scene in the haberdashery where Torrence, as the hard-boiled old river pilot, buys his collegiate son a hat. That scene alone is worth the price of admission.

Judge, June 2, 1928

END OF ST. PETERSBURG

THE RUSSIAN Soviet government presents a picture of the Russian Revolution that may honestly be called a masterpiece. *End of St. Petersburg* is subtle propaganda for the Soviet government, but it is also the best directed and most beautiful movie I have seen in months. From the beginning, the picture moves with the slow, sombre tread of a bleeding giant stalking across great stretches of land, ladling molten streams of lead, forging cannons, and uprooting trees and buildings with blind, invincible strength.

End of St. Petersburg, for the first time, catches the dumb agony of the oppressed peasantry of Russia, and with grand strokes the picture of their slow, ponderous rebellion is painted in beautiful black and white on the screen.

These Russian movie people know what they are doing. With the exception of the pictures Murnau has done and the pictures Vidor has demonstrated he would like to do, *End of St. Petersburg* shows you the power of the medium more impressively than any recent American productions have demonstrated. There is no place here for "talking sequences."

There are places where the story seems a bit stupid, at least in comparison with our industrial practices, and in these sequences the Soviet object lesson is obvious, but there is no dramatic situation in the story that is vitiated by propaganda or "box office" interpolation, so that the objection is of little value.

There is no comedy relief, no sweet little girl who is the toast of the Soviet Army; there is nothing but grim reality painted in the most gorgeous colors you have ever seen in a movie. There is nothing funny about hunger, mud, cold steel, or ignorance. There is one short scene in the jail which is amusing, and it was startling to hear the audience let down for the moment and snap hungrily for the laugh.

As a history of the rise of the Soviet government, this movie is romantic fiction, but as a movie *End of St. Petersburg* is dramatic, thrilling, and beautiful. It wipes away the memory of the Hollywood trash that emasculates the power which can really be obtained with the movie camera once it is given into the hands of unhampered, intelligent men.

Judge, June 23, 1928

THE RACKET

SOMBRE, restrained, and convincing, the movie adaptation of Bartlett Cormack's melodrama, "The Racket," is unusually good.

It has as its villain not a Jean Lafitte who quotes Anatole France, but an illiterate gangster who has gained political control of a corrupt metropolis through his bloody and successful evasion of the Eighteenth Amendment. The hero is not a booted Northwest Mountie who carries a picture of his mother glued to his pearl-handled revolver, but a veteran Irish cop who refuses to allow a vicious crew of post-war killers to drive him from his profession.

This is one of those movies that comes along once in a trans-atlantic flight. The play was unusual in that it was a "one-woman" play, and it is to the everlasting credit of the author that he did not let his heroine become camera shy and change her from a lady of the sidewalks to a golden-haired Little Nell when he adapted his manuscript. Hard-boiled she remains.

Having seen the play and regarded it as one of the best melo-dramas of recent years, it is difficult to review the movie with an unprejudiced eye, but it is possible to report that Director Lewis Milestone followed the sequences of the play as faithfully as possible and that naturally the few defects of the play again manifest themselves. The most prominent of these, as was pointed out by George Jean Nathan, was the role of the cub reporter who is sent out by his paper to cover the biggest story in the city. However, against the faithfulness of the rest of the plot, this defect becomes a triviality.

The role of the villain, Scarzi, was given a marvelous performance by Edward Robinson on the stage, and Lewis Wolheim does it full justice on the screen. He is the outstanding character in the picture. Credit must be given to Director Milestone for the unusual restraint put upon his cast, and they have good accounts of themselves, with the exception of the two men assigned to do the reporters; they were evidently so stirred with the thought that they were the comedy relief that they felt it necessary to pop up before the camera at every opportunity with all the coy gaiety of a couple of chorus boys hoofing on their first job.

Judge, July 28, 1928

Peroration No. 1
THE STILLBORN ART

I HAVE read a dozen essays published during the past year assuring the public that the movies are laboring in the birth agony of a great art. Against these statements other prophets have submitted in type that movie houses are inhabited only by people who vote the Democratic ticket, and that the entire industry does not amount to a Bruce Barton editorial.

I have seen over three hundred movies within eighteen months, and I suspect any man who proclaims we are on the verge of christening a new art of being the sort of cluck who thinks the Marines were sent to Nicaragua to teach the native Boy Scouts how to build bird houses. But only a fool could dismiss the movies as a passing annoyance.

To say that under the present management they are cheap and vulgar, that they cannot possibly furnish satisfactory entertainment for erudite society, that they have become the most vulgar and nauseating manifestation of our economic condition—all these statements can be accepted, but it is ignorance to dismiss lightly the strength of any influence as financially and psychologically powerful as the American movie.

It is quite possible that the perfect movie has never been made, that it is an infant art struggling with childish gestures for expression, but big business has forced the producers to become efficient, and that pressure has resulted in a startling uniformity. Mechanically, artistically, and financially there is every indication that those people who have felt the dramatic possibilities and boundaries of the motion picture as an adult diversion are going to suffer gross disappointments for many years. The movie has arrived. It can create robust entertainment. But right now it is throttled by all the inhibitions of democracy. The new art has been born, but it lacked expert obstetrical care.

There was a time when you could indict movies for obvious faults in production—bad lighting, amateur photography, obvious technical errors. People still went to see movies as a mechanical curiosity in those days. Now, however, a great host of well-trained cameramen, scenario writers, and directors have made it possible for the producers to chart out production schedules for a year at a time. They can almost count on certain movies with stars to bring so much profit in certain key cities.

They plan a number of big features during a certain period of time, with a greater number of "programme" pictures to fill in the gaps. The features are given the dignity of two-a-day performances in a few large cities and then, with this prestige, are installed in the big houses of the country. Certainly, with this procedure bringing greater and greater financial return, it is not likely that the producers are going to change their ways just because a wounded spirit writes vicious notes claiming that it isn't artistic. And while this may be merely one period of the evolution of the industry, it shows every sign of being a long period, and I for one am not altruistic enough to worry about the art that may be handed down to my grandchildren. It's enough to worry about handing down grandchildren.

A summary of three hundred of the best pictures exhibited in these last eighteen months convincingly demonstrates this uniformity of production. It seems certain that this will become more and more permanent. The affluence of the giant companies has allowed them to corral the best technicians, directors, writers, and gag men from all over the world. So many American pictures were being exhibited in France, England, and Germany that those countries had to place an embargo on the importation of American films. Not to be defeated, the American companies then established their own producing units in those various countries, with the result that today there are American companies on foreign soil making pictures with the same editorial attitude that is assumed by Hollywood. That attitude may be hastily summarized: the greatest amount of "hooey" for the greatest number of people.

The movies belong to Big Business, and Big Business, of course, is in the hands of God. Who makes movies? In America, Metro-Goldwyn-Mayer, Paramount, United Artists, First National,

F. B. O., William Fox, Universal, Pathé, De Mille, and about one hundred and twenty small producers. If you are at all familiar with movies, the names of the big companies here listed will be familiar to you—in two years I have not seen more than one or two feature pictures that were made, distributed, or exhibited by any other organizations. In 1927, according to the Film Daily, there were 743 "feature" pictures released, and of these, 135 were made by "independents"—companies other than those named above. Not one of the 135 had a national star in it. I did not see or hear of one of these pictures ever reaching a good theatre in New York City.

We therefore have an art form controlled by a handful of corporations. The Paramount Company has now been given a "cease and desist" order by the Federal Trade Commission for practicing what is designated as "blind booking" and for operating in restraint of trade. There have been several conferences, but so far the Trade Commission has not put Mr. Zukor or Mr. Lasky in jail. The complaint in the case was originally filed on August 30, 1921, was amended on February 14, 1923, and hearings and agreements dragged on for over four years, with 30,000 pages of testimony being finally included in the record.

Without going into the involutions of the financial condition of the industry, this generalization can be supported: fewer than a dozen American movie companies have the financial strength to dominate the production and manufacture of movies, not only in this country, but in Germany, France, and England. (A desperate measure recently introduced in France may exclude all American pictures from that country. It is estimated that there are 50,000 movie theatres in the world. Of these, 21,000 are American, and of these, the largest city theatres—if not actually owned or controlled by the aforenamed companies—are dependent upon their pictures for existence.)

Yet the movie is supposed to be an art form. Imagine twelve publishing houses directing the style of all the authors in the country, exerting a great influence on all book dealers, and even imposing American methods of writing upon foreign publishers and authors! I am not accusing the big companies of monopoly. The

Federal Trade Commission has already done this. But I do think this indicates the power of a set form of manufacture that shows signs of continuing for years.

At mere mention of the movies, sour journalists jerk a thumb in the direction of the Woolworth Building and hiss "Wall Street" with knowing inflection. True, when Wall Street lays hands on a half-billion dollars' worth of corporation, it is not long ere the voting control comes home wagging its stockholders behind it. But what difference will it make in the conception of the movie if Wall Street does get financial control? Efficiency and standardization do not mean entertainment and good taste. If one cameraman does the work of two, and Lily Le Grande wears a cheap $10,000 Paris frock in six movies instead of one, will that make the movie any stronger? Mr. Mellon does not hire Gutzon Borglum to make molds for his aluminum kettles simply because the company is an efficient and prosperous concern.

Censorship militates in favor of emasculated uniformity. The films have attained such financial proportions that all professional reformers and censors have turned with brightened eyes to the golden streets of Hollywood. Always troubled by the censors, the movies are now in that state of maidenly apprehension so typical of all corporations in the United States. Every great utility these days has a flock of Harvard law graduates poring over publicity bulletins and vice presidents' speeches, for fear some careless fellow will let loose the remark that the company is actually making a good income and leave the way wide open for an investigation by Senator Walsh or one of our few irritable legislators. The movies, constantly before the public eye, are even more afraid of the censorship bogey, and "Bishop" Hays must throw lilies of the valley at every species of organization that comes to town, from the National Board of Review to the American Association of Veterinarians.

"If foreigners favor American movies, then aren't American movies superior?" They are, but this is what happens: If a German company makes a financially successful picture, the director and actors are offered huge sums to come to Hollywood. (The UFA Company in Germany turns out some excellent pictures. Paramount owns some interest in the company now, and employs its directors and stars—Emil Jannings being the most famous of the expatriate Germans.) The best-trained movie men in the world go to Hollywood. Immediately their work is held in by the producer. Their work lacks "guts" because of box-office censorship. These feature movies have uniformity, of course, because the directors are too clever to botch their job. And there you are!

I take the liberty of quoting a letter from Mr. Robert Herring, the astute critic of the London Mercury: "It is so depressing to see pictures like *Sunrise* and *The Way of All Flesh*, that try to please Europe by aping its tricks and reconstructing its life. What we want from Germany is Germany. And what we seem to get from the two most vital countries in the world is American-Germany and German-America. It is a pity, for after all only America can give that something we need very much. It seems to me that a dead uniformity will result from its 'internationalism.' " From this letter you can see that our uniform production has already registered in England.

I also quote from Terry Ramsaye's authoritative work, "A Million and One Nights": "The arrival of the World War in 1914 halted British and European production activities and left the evolution of the art and the industry alike to America alone. The motion picture was thus delivered over to America at the beginning of its greatest development, the feature drama . . . The opening of the world market is carrying the American rivalries into struggles of exploitation overseas . . . The American position is overwhelmingly strong with the foundation of uninterrupted growth and a continuously prosperous domestic patronage. Also, since the American producer has always served a polyglot and extremely diverse population, his products have automatically evolved with a certain innate internationalism and a catholicity which tends to make them world-market merchandise."

Who goes to the movies in America? Everybody. An army of clerks go and take it seriously, and occasionally we all go just because there is nothing else to do. This, in a measure, explains the fantastical growth of the movies in America. Go, go, go! We must kill time somehow. There are no beer gardens. There are no public concerts except for the esoteric and affluent few. The roads are too crowded to make riding a pleasure. Who wants to sit at home and play bridge every night? The radio batteries have run down. Let's go to a movie. It's probably rotten, but hurry up, let's go. At least some members of the movie audience feel a lack of depth in the entertainment they witness. The ordinary movie patrons do not unanimously applaud every production they see. But they go. Night after night, they go to be lulled into the complacent lethargy of stuffed toads.

The masses certainly are worthy of a higher type of entertainment than they are given by the Hollywood prelates. But who gives a damn? Not the members of a democracy, when they are fed, watered, and amused.

I overheard two men discussing the theatre one night on a train moving west out of New York. A Middle Western buyer was eulogizing the movie, *Ben Hur,* which he and his wife had seen in the city. "It's the greatest thing I ever saw," he rhapsodized, "and the stage play was nothing compared to it. Why, in the play they had only two or three slaves—they had 20,000 in the picture." This is a sound comment on democracy's fine art. In no other country in the world would this seem so important. "More Camels sold this year than ever before—more General Motors cars put out— the 30,000,000th Ford is being made today—there were 20,000 slaves in that picture"—a logical sequence of national approbation. Anything that is big must be good.

The movie is the most convenient form of entertainment in the world. It does not cost much (although, at that, it costs a great deal more than it should) to see two well-informed inhale-exhale artists exhibit their particular technique of necking, and the comfortable seats and the banal music have a soporific effect on a public that seeks relief from its own restlessness. You can be bored with more comfort at a movie than anywhere else.

The religious attitude of the movie is another distinct symptom of our democracy. I have never seen a movie that entertained any religious concept (and about three out of ten do have some suggestion of the Creator) which suggested any belief other than that there is a personal God, and the inference has always been that His chief business is to keep tabs on the virginity of the nation. This God is usually represented by some superstitious demonstration, such as was displayed by His electrical dexterity in *The Ten Commandments*, or by the earthquake He sent in *Old San Francisco*, or by the life that was saved by a Catholic medallion in *Seventh Heaven*—all "feature" productions. Also typical of a nation boasting religious tolerance, all other religions—Muhammadanism, Buddhism, Confucianism, etc.—are held up to hilarious ridicule and, in the more serious productions, stern disapproval.

Ignoring the complacent majority, then, there are, perhaps, a great many people who realize that the movie in its present development offers real emotional entertainment, that there are men in Hollywood who know how to direct and photograph pictures as stimulating as good novels or a well-shouldered sonata. There have been exhibits which were encouraging. *The Big Parade*, *Variety*, *Sunrise*, and *Underworld* belong in this group. Still, examine them carefully. With the exception of *Sunrise*, not one of these movies had a distinct artistic or mechanical superiority to the best movies of three years ago. They were simply smooth, uniform productions.

The Big Parade was written directly for the movies by Laurence Stallings. He wrote it with a definite conception of the limitations and advantages of his medium. The producers looked upon it and declared it good, and Stallings was fortunate in having King Vidor direct it. But before the movie was shown to the public, a scene was inserted from the stage play, "What Price Glory," and a silly, illogical ending stuck on despite the protests of Stallings.

Variety was noteworthy for its simple, moving story, for its photography and acting, but by the time it reached New York it was vitiated into fair entertainment; and when it was sent out of that center of culture, it was castrated by censorship—mostly self-imposed by the producers—until it was an utterly absurd piece of work.

Underworld was written by a former Chicago police reporter, directed by one of the Chaplin-trained directors in Hollywood, and ably supported by as good a cast as he could scrape together in the entire colony. The Paramount Company, it has been rumored, considered *Underworld* a failure as a picture and was on the point of dismissing the scoffed author and the hard-working Mr. Von Sternberg, the director. Public opinion changed the opinion of the Paramount overlords and they gave Von Sternberg a medal, some speeches, and $10,000. Before the picture even left Hollywood, the directors had changed the ending originally conceived by its author, Ben Hecht; they stuck on a concluding caption to the effect that "you can't beat the law," and allowed this lily-scented episode to climax a very forceful and intelligent motion picture.

Sunrise, with its synchronized musical score, is the best conception of a motion picture that has been shown in this country. This is due solely to the director—F. W. Murnau—a keen, cultured man with an artist's eye. The first fifteen minutes of this picture are perfect—then a silly Prohibition gag is inserted, an absolutely inconsistent conclusion grafted to the story, and, in general, a great piece of work "goes to hell" because, we may presume, the producers believed the original idea would be too stark and real for a chocolate-sundae audience. The picture was a real tragedy to me. From the start one felt the expert grasp of the artist who was directing the picture. The photography was breathtaking. Then, without warning, the grasp was loosened and palpable "box-office" scenes inserted. It was nauseating. Even in its present form, *Sunrise* is grand entertainment, because Mr. Murnau is no slipshod artist; but it just missed being a masterpiece. Here is a typical case. If one is to believe press notices, Murnau is making pictures to please Americans (i.e., his employer William Fox) and not to please Mr. Murnau. I have no great scorn of best sellers, but when the majority of directors are little more than quick-witted shoe clerks with little background and less erudition, it seems hopeless when a cultured artist is compelled to turn out a piece of work inconsistently straddling stark drama and loose box-office values.

The pictures I have described are among the few exhibited within the past year that have stood above the run of programme movies, always excepting animal and travel pictures and newsreels. None of these described was consistently great because all were distorted by their proprietors to fit a Hollywood opinion of what a movie audience should be allowed to see. Outstanding exceptions are Douglas Fairbanks and Charles Chaplin. These men labor long and patiently to achieve magnificent effects. They know their trade and they are interested more in sincere effort than in turning out carloads of movies. However, they are wealthy enough to gamble. And Fairbanks has made nothing in recent years that equaled *The Thief of Bagdad.*

For several years critics have maintained that as long as movie companies make pictures aimed at the common denominator of the mass audiences required in the cathedrals of the motion pictures, we shall have celluloid drivel imposed upon us, but that a little movie theatre, with negligible overhead cost and a discriminating clientele, could support important movies. The little movie theatre has existed in various forms in New York City and at the present time it approaches the artistic level of an Alice Foote Mac-Dougall Coffee Shop. These theatres show foreign pictures that are sent over—to judge by their worth—for six dollars a dozen. The only American pictures shown at these rendezvous of Bronx intelligentsia (as the management of two of these little theatres admitted recently) are odd pieces of film so badly done that a plebeian cathedral of the movies would not be able to fill the orchestra pit with them.

In other words, the three little theatres in New York City—no matter how high their original purpose—find they cannot buy movies from independent producers that even approach the smooth performances of the big companies, and they now depend on Greenwich Village poets and department store clerks with artistic leanings for their livelihood. In fact, the Fifth Avenue Playhouse and the 55th Street Cinema have become notorious with reviewers for their terribly cheap and affected programmes.

This, then, is the condition as I see it in Hollywood. The movies and the majority of the movie houses are controlled by a small group of financiers. The best men in the industry are employed by these companies. If they struck out on their own, there would be no theatre circuit of any size to buy their stuff. The American companies are so strong they are driving all foreign competition to the wall, despite the efforts of foreign governments. People in America have nothing else to do, so even with the certainty of being bored by inconsequential stories, sickly sentimentality, and boorish ethics, they go to the movies. Hence monopoly and censorship will hold stories and situations within the gentle limits of Mother Goose rhymes for many years.

For the future, there will be larger and larger movie houses giving programmes of third-rate vaudeville and harmless, vitiated motion pictures, unless a nauseated public stands up and roars, "We won't stand for it!" Just at present it would seem that our national capacity for boredom is unlimited. In a country as powerful, restless, and capable as the United States it would be folly to say progress is impossible in any mechanical or artistic field; but for the reasons I have presented, I believe the movies will go no further until one of the following incidents changes the situation:

(1) the return of saloons or beer gardens, or the discovery of a like diversion to relieve people of the driving necessity of the movie;

(2) the development of new methods by men in Germany or England or France, who will scorn the offers of Hollywood and sell their pictures to independent theatre owners;

(3) the development and merging of television and photography of sound, plus brilliant direction, into an entirely new art form; or

(4) the development of a movie company, with powerful backing, that will make pictures for little theatres with no desire for immediate profit.

The Forum, September, 1928

THE PATRIOT

W HEN you are really logy from seeing reel after reel of tasteless movies, it is flying in the face of gratitude to find fault with a picture so superior in every way as *The Patriot*.

This picture provides one of those interludes, so rare in our cathedrals of the moving celluloid, which allows you to sit back and experience a lusty satisfaction at the performance, unmarred by a single note of stereotyped Hollywood practice.

Mr. Neumann probably never thought of Emil Jannings when he wrote this play around Paul, Czar of Russia, but I think even an author would experience a healthy glow of enthusiasm at the grand manner in which Jannings bellows and roars his way through the characterization of the mad son of Catherine the Great.

From the moment the big fellow sticks his leering countenance around the massive door of the throne room, every other item in the picture retreats into subdued relief. He waddles through the cold marble halls with the evil gusto of a child of the devil, a trained bear set on the heights of Olympus, a clumsy-pawed, mischievous gorilla given control of the universe.

It is movie tradition that successful box-office "types" are repeated until they grow stale, and up to this picture Mr. Jannings has not been permitted to do much except march ponderously down stairways and through alleys with the same Wagnerian tread which brought him fame in *Variety* and *The Last Laugh*.

However, in *The Patriot*, Mr. Jannings giggles, he sticks out his tongue at justice, he romps with the destinies of a country. The part was brilliantly written in the play, and Jannings plays it clear to the bone.

What credit does not belong to Jannings should be attributed to the deft hand of Ernst Lubitsch, the director.

Herr Lubitsch, who unquestionably is one of the greatest directors in the movies, maintains an atmosphere of austerity throughout the story, and under his supervision Lewis Stone does the best work it has ever been my pleasure to witness from that gentleman.

There was a fault, imposed by the company. (Well, you didn't think I could go on being nice indefinitely, did you?) After the picture had been completely finished, so I understand, sound sequences were added. It was stupid on the part of Paramount. Just because it is a current selling device does not mean that it lends dramatic interest to a job that was brilliantly directed and performed.

However, the raucous interference of the sound sequences does not enter into the picture frequently enough to give you more than a flicker of annoyance. It's a pleasure to recommend a picture with the character of *The Patriot*.

Judge, September 8, 1928

THE CAMERAMAN

THERE is that old bromide which reads that "A man who would analyze wit and humor can understand neither," so I shall not be too incisive concerning Buster Keaton, but I recommend his picture, *The Cameraman*.

Indubitably, the picture is not up to the standard of Keaton's earlier pictures, *The Navigator*, *The General*, and *College*. He has gone to work for another company and its production has not come up to the well-polished excellency of the comedies turned out by Keaton's own outfit.

But, uncritical or not, this wooden-faced lad does not need a story, a leading lady, or a new gag to be entertaining. Give him six square feet of space, and he'll do things with his eyes, hands, and feet that are neat, spontaneous, and funny.

There is one ace scene in *The Cameraman*, as there usually is in a Keaton movie, in which the hero plays a baseball game by himself to the cold austerity of the deserted Yankee Stadium.

The idea is amusing, but Keaton, by virtue of knowing the art of pantomime, peoples the diamond with uniformed athletes, fills the concrete tiers with shirt-sleeved fans, and so animates the picture you can even see Mr. Rickard's trained troop of surly morons, whom he jovially calls ushers, leading late customers to wrong seats.

Because of the love interest, the movie is long-winded and the last sequence is very labored and dull. But, if only for the baseball game and the scene wherein the cop, a comical-faced fellow named Harry Gribbon, and Keaton sit in the driving rain and test each other's reflexes, I recommend it.

Judge, October 13, 1928

SINGING FOOL

Despite the gold tickets, the rotogravure advertising in the Sunday papers, despite the battery of searchlights at Times Square and the reserves on guard at the Winter Garden entrance, despite the great floral wreaths that transformed the lobby of the old theatre into an undertaker's nightmare, despite the luxurious background of the most be-studded and be-ermined movie audience I have ever seen, despite the personal appearance of any number of Broadway stars, in the face of one of the oldest plots known to the industry, and much to my surprise, *Singing Fool* is a success; in fact, the great financial return on *The Jazz Singer*, Jolson's first talking picture, accelerated the talking pictures on their chaotic career. And, there, too, it was the man and not the story that put the picture over.

Vitaphone has better reproduction in *Singing Fool*, and Jolson loses the self-consciousness he showed at times in his first movie, so that his second screen effort is a much smoother performance. The story, of course, is terrible, and it has no excuse except as a thread on which to string the songs he sings. Fortunately, there are many.

If you doubt that Jolson is a great artist in his own field, stick around until the big scene at the end of the picture, where he does a Laugh, Clown, Laugh act—the hammiest trick in the theatre. (If Leoncavallo is still living, he probably cries in his beer every time he remembers that he wrote "I Pagliacci," the favorite movie opera.) The situation, which was used in his first picture, calls for Jolson to go on and sing when his heart is broken over the loss of his only child. Obvious and tedious as the climax is, when the black-face comedian stands before the camera and sings "Sonny Boy" you know the man is greater, somehow, than the situation, the story, or the movie. Which wouldn't be difficult under any circumstances.

However, it does go over, and I defy you to conceive of a more difficult test for a singer than standing before the unresponsive eye of a camera and creating the illusion with a sentimental ballad (on sale in the lobby as you go out) that his heart is breaking.

There is so much sadness and strife in the story that the big climax seems a bit weak, but I recommend as unqualified entertainment the bull-fighter's song and the story of the bullfrog that sent the turtle for some aspirin, as told by Jolson to his son.

Now for the moral. I'm sure you're all tired of hearing about the talking movies, but teacher will dismiss the class early if you'll let me get this idea to you. As I pointed out in *The Jazz Singer* review, singing does not disturb the illusion of the movie, but when a voice crackles out at you, unassisted by even a faint orchestration, it jars your senses. It jerks you completely away from the scene and the feeling of the situation and makes the screen appear gray and flat.

There are several dialogue sequences early in *Singing Fool*, but there is an orchestra playing in the background and this music, faint as it is, carries you along with the story. However, when Jolson steps out on the floor and makes an announcement, the sudden lone sound of his voice immediately rips the curtain of illusion off the screen and makes it a flat, colorless thing, animated by a not-too-attractive voice.

Against that, listen to the bullfrog story. This is the best synchronization I have ever heard; the music is written for the dialogue, a low woodwind accompaniment, and Jolson tells the story in perfect time. It's a marvelous scene in that the atmosphere, the music, and the story are in time and tune. Here may be the real future of the talking devices: blank verse written in time to orchestration. *Sunrise* had everything except the dialogue.

Such dialogue could fit very well into a fantasy such as *The Thief of Bagdad*, the most beautiful picture ever made, in my opinion, where ordinary dialogue would be dull and puny.

Thank you for your patience. Class dismissed.

Judge, October 20, 1928

HALLELUJAH

AFTER tearing my collar off and yelling myself hoarse over *Hallelujah*, I thought I had better go back and see it again, just to make sure. Besides, I read a review in Time that annoyed me.

Said the anonymous critic of Time: "Before the end of this picture you get the idea that King Vidor, who wrote and directed it, does not know much about Negroes but that he has guessed and reasoned out a lot. His story, simple yet sophisticated, does not go as deep into the way a black man's mind works as, for instance, Eugene O'Neill went in 'Emperor Jones.' "

This is the polished rhetoric and incisive comment typical of movie criticism in a country that produces sixty percent of the world's supply.

Before the end of the picture, I not only got the idea that King Vidor knew his subject but that he had an extraordinary understanding of the motivating instincts of his characters. Vidor chose a robust, kindly plantation Negro for his main character. All plantation Negroes are no more like Zeke than all Baptist ministers are like Elmer Gantry. However, Elmer Gantry is the loud-mouthed and cheap dramatization of a loud-mouthed and cheap group of apostles. Zeke is the simple, superstitious, and savage epitome of the unspoiled, healthy plantation Negro.

The revival scenes in *Hallelujah* are not typical revival scenes, but they were not created out of fantasy either. I have seen a hundred Negro services, and the only two that resembled the movie ceremonies were Holy Roller camp meetings in the Southwest. They were, however, the most exciting and primitive orgies I had ever seen. If you think Vidor "guessed" his movie scenes, then Conrad guessed at the characters of seamen.

To quote again—"The story did not go as deep as O'Neill's 'Emperor Jones.'" This should rank as one of the silliest statements of 1929. With the exception of "In Abraham's Bosom," what play of Negro life ever written in America has even touched the root springs of the Negro spirit except "Emperor Jones," a great play written by our greatest dramatist? In other words, Time holds that because *Hallelujah*, a movie operetta, did not contain the depth of that one great dramatization of a Negro, it was a poor job. Under that ruling, "The Sacred Flame" was a cheap play because it was not as stark as "Ghosts," and "Desire Under the Elms" was a vaudeville act because it was not as incisive as "Strange Interlude."

Some jaundiced instinct seems to restrain the boys and girls from tipping their hats when a great man comes along. I think Vidor in his casting, his music, his story, and his photography, created the greatest dramatization of the Negro as he still exists outside the Harlem culture belt that ever can be done with the movie form. The movietone was the best I have ever heard. I have yet to see a better job of acting than that performed by Daniel Haynes.

Reviewers of the Tribune and the Evening World wrote well and truthfully of *Hallelujah*. The Times, as usual, left one in complete doubt as to whether the reporter was writing about a movie or the Negro problem in Dutch Guiana. The substitute critics for the Sun and the Morning World exhausted their space in an account of the Harlem opening-night audience, and the usually judicious gentleman of the Evening Post said that "in only one short sequence is the film anything less than intensely absorbing. As drama it is episodic and tends toward biography. The conclusion is weak and lacking in emphasis . . . on three or four occasions the sound mechanisms have been so adroitly manipulated as to bring stunning climaxes." He then turned to an account of the story, with no further statement of good, poor, or superb.

It remains for the public and those artists who know their composition to thank Vidor. The producers will only if it comes back in dividends, and most of the critics are too tired.

Judge, September 21, 1929

Sunrise

End of St. Petersburg
Singing Fool   *The Patriot*

Hallelujah

The Thirties

NEWSREELS

ABOUT three months ago, a lawyer asked me why the movies put so little news in the newsreels. I didn't know, so I went knocking from door to door trying to find the answer. I discovered, for one thing, that the boys in the newsreel business are just about as tough as any old-time gang of door-crashing reporters who ever lived. The story of "how the pictures of the Bremen fliers at Greenley Island came through" is an epic of news adventure. It cost one company $85,000 to get 1,000 feet of film to New York City, including a plane that was wrecked by a rival company's sabotage, and a cameraman who was beaten unconscious by the alert employees of a well-known chain-newspaper owner. Obviously, the newsreel boys are willing to get news. Why, then, didn't they get sound pictures of the Hall-Mills trial, the Sinclair trial, or any other real news story that has occupied front-page newspaper space? There is only one answer I could take back to the lawyer: "Will Hays won't let them."

Mr. Hays has boasted several times that his boys have never, never shown anything as pernicious as murder, graft, or back-room politics on their undefiled screens. And, when you come right down to it, a sound reel of Mr. Hays testifying before the Senate Investigating Committee in regard to some bonds he handled several years ago might possibly arouse some dark doubts in the shadowless minds of the great movie public; it might even cause a murmur of unpleasantness to reach the ears of the Republican party, and even while it might be news, it just wouldn't be good sense.

Therefore, an all-newsreel program at the Newsreel Theatre in New York City has the following vital subjects to present, according to the Herald Tribune: "Dr. Adolph Lorenz, the Viennese surgeon, gives a short talk on bloodless surgery and expresses his hope that disease will yet be prevented; Colonel and Mrs. Charles A. Lindbergh are shown leaving Curtiss Field on a flight to the Pacific Coast, and W. H. Bowles, of Punta Loma, California, may be seen establishing the American record for gliders after remaining in the air more than two hours.

"The wedding of the Aga Khan, Indian prince and sportsman, and Mlle. Andrée Josephine Carron is also depicted, and a scene from Palestine shows Jews and Arabs trading peacefully once more while British troops patrol the streets. There is a shot showing the English Channel during a recent storm with monstrous waves pounding against the side of a large steamer in mid-channel; it also shows coast towns with the streets flooded and persons using rowboats as means of travel. Another scene shows Horace Liveright judging a contest of intellect between girls from Hunter College and chorus girls. The Hunter girls won.

"In addition, one may see and hear Health Commissioner Shirley W. Wynne warning against bad liquor, fancy skating at an ice carnival, 3,000 children singing at a festival in Rome, a market scene in Morocco, primitive life in Hawaii, Jack Johnson leading a jazz band, and Ralph Greenleaf regaining his pocket billiard crown in Detroit."

This morning's headlines inform me that there are three captive rum ships and three corpses lying in state in Rhode Island, laid out by government machine-gun bullets. There are at least two other similar stories that, photographed and presented in a theatre, might bring the grim facts of Prohibition a little closer to home.

But indubitably Mr. Hays is wise in preferring to give us pleasant little glimpses of jazz bands and foreign lands. After all, if the public was too well informed, it might start something, and the idea of a nation in action is always unpleasant to the Hayses of our land, who much prefer to leave the problems of humanity in the hands of God and a committee.

Judge, January 18, 1930

ANNA CHRISTIE

THE ADVENT of Greta Garbo, with sound, was hailed by her owners as an occasion comparable to the second coming of Sarah Bernhardt. The public was persuaded without difficulty, and the tall, monotonous Swedish star, by the more or less childish trick of learning the English language, has brought the box-office receipts piling in. The occasion was celebrated with *Anna Christie*, based on a play of many seasons ago, written by Eugene O'Neill. Some liberty was taken with the manuscript, so that there is little of the harsh but poetic reality of the early O'Neill retained in the new celluloid version. (The play was given a silent treatment with passable success several years ago.) There are not many alterations, but, in the usual movie manner, the plot is explained in words of two syllables by an extraneous thousand feet or so tacked on before the scene that originally opened the play. This scene was, and is, the most effective and simple bit in the manuscript. It is a dialogue between a young and a worn member of the world's oldest profession.

The two movie audiences I sat with chose to regard the show as a comedy, and I believe their reaction was right. The effective buffoonery of Marie Dressler overclouded her genuine and understanding portrayal of a South Street wharf rat. Charles Bickford tore into his characterization of a simple seaman with so much gusto that he was regarded as a vaudeville Irish comedian. Miss Garbo gave an original and surprising interpretation of the heroine.

George Marion, as the announcer who steps to the fore and mumbles about the "ol' davil sea," acted as though he were giving an elaborate bedtime story over the radio. But it is Miss Garbo who brought the audience to the theatre, and who, necessarily, is the subject under discussion.

I do not see that there is any other way to discuss most movies except in terms of personalities. Here you have a story that is an early effort of a master craftsman. It was adapted for the movies years ago. As is true of a hundred movies every month, there is nothing deep, profound, or unique enough about the plot to dig your toes into. Yet I do not see that my own opinion of Greta Garbo is of any more use to you than a passing comment on the hat-check girl. I do know that if you insist on calling her an actress, we then have something to bicker over, even though I would be hard put to give you my definition of that craft. Before her first talking role, Miss Garbo impressed me as an indolent young lady with an unusual figure and absolutely no warmth or color, much less any indication of emotional depth or craft. In *Anna Christie*, she produces a deep, monotonous, but humorous voice. And that was surprising. It dispelled forever the "mysterious lady" personality and left her a young lady who was seriously trying to understand her job, but who was much too easy-going and goodnatured to get a sweat up over it.

My opinion of her ability is really based on her work in a movie called *Love*, adapted with little success from "Anna Karenina." Her monkeyshines with John Gilbert were of no importance, but in one scene she was called upon to enter, at great loss of pride, the nursery of her son, whom she had forsaken. The young lady simply came in the room and played with the toys as though she were passing the time until tea. I am not a director, and I specify no rules, but she walked in and out of that set with no more expression or concern on her face than a clam. I don't ask a great deal of calisthenics with my drama, but I like to get something of a show for my money. As I am not interested in movie figures or scandal, I have yet to feel even the slightest curiosity in the Swedish celebrity. Audibility has given her a good humor. But that doesn't make an actress capable of projecting the hopeless despair of a Minnesota prostitute isolated on a coal barge with a paranoiac father.

The director, Clarence Brown, should share most of the blame for the weakness of *Anna Christie* in that he cast a girl whose every gesture indicated a charming school-girl conception of tragedy for a difficult part, and for that reason I suggest that you see Miss Garbo for yourself.

Judge, April 5, 1930

HIGH TREASON

PROPAGANDA of any kind is dull, whether it is about war, peace, naval disarmament, or polar discovery. The most obvious explanation is that it is humorless and without form. A British company has produced a movie called *High Treason*, and while it is an imaginative and interesting piece of work, the lack of reality, the solemn, humorless spirit of its hero and heroine vitiate the drama of the story. There is no reason to believe that the leader of a peace army would be any less thick-headed than a member of the War Office. It may be that peace agitators in England are of a higher caliber than our own specimens, but to dramatize them as shining knights without fault is to make them more than dull and uninteresting characters.

High Treason has the best camera picture of the world of the future since *Metropolis*. The action takes place in 1940; television and aviation have changed the habits of the world. There are two great political states—the "Atlantic States" and the "Federated States of Europe." The film opens with the most reasonable conception in the plot, a fight between the Atlantic and Federated border guards over a rum car (the Atlantic States, of course, being dry). This incident precipitates an international crisis and the dramatic interest is sustained by a careful presentation of the actual business of war in the future. The women have been conscripted, according to *High Treason*, and they march to their area command to take up munitions work as soon as the Federated States receive mobilization orders. The major units of the world armies are bombing each other, a reasonable forecast.

The leader of the peace army, a world organization, and his daughter attempt to prevent mobilization. The daughter is in love with the head of the Federated air unit. There is a silly and unnecessary story of an international munitions intrigue. It is not silly to presume that munition manufacturers might agitate for war, but in *High Treason* they are made to act and talk like a Brisbane editorial. Their work is of little importance. The television announcements, the meetings in New York and London have the verisimilitude of war, and the scenes of the bombing squadrons and the munition factories are grim and realistic enough to set you thinking.

After a vain effort to prevent the citizens of the Federated States from obeying the mobilization order, the president of the peace army calls on the president of his country. The Federated chief is to declare for or against war "to the world" at midnight. The peace leader consults the president in his private office. He is told the council has decided upon war. At midnight the world tunes in its television sets. The peace president steps before the instrument and announces that the president of the Federated States has decided to submit to arbitration. The startled Federated chief shoots at the televison set and the peace leader turns and shoots the president. He again announces that the war has been called off. Despite public sympathy, the peace president is tried and convicted for murder in the English courts.

The thorough technical work in *High Treason* makes it easily the best movie an English producer has ever shown in this country. There is no petty sex theme. War is the villain, peace is the hero. The saintly make-up and character of the peace leader is a dull piece of business, but the theme overrides its protagonist. Considering the usual run of movies, *High Treason* is a superior job and well worth your time. But for no reason that they will divulge, the state censors of New York and Pennsylvania have refused to license *High Treason*, and will not let it be shown in any form in their states!

Either they oppose peace, either they resent the un-American idea that an Englishman could head a peace army or, more reason-

ably, they altruistically and for no filthy profit to themselves oppose competition to Hollywood. If you are a member of either of
these great commonwealths, perhaps you can get your Senator to
find the reason for this autocratic condemnation.

Judge, May 10, 1930

BLOTTO

I AM LATE getting around to Laurel and Hardy. I always suspect
all clichés. I have never joined the Amos 'n' Andy school, and I
did not belong to the now deceased Moran-and-Mack league. However, without a doubt, the two-reel comedies of Laurel and Hardy
are the funniest and the best directed short movies being made today. The director, James Parrott, has developed a peculiar method-
ical, simple routine for his comedy team. The last one I saw,
Blotto, had very few gags and not much of a story. But the gags
were pulled so deliberately and with such finesse, I wonder that
Mr. Parrott does not establish a new school of movie direction.

Judge, May 10, 1930

ALL QUIET ON THE WESTERN FRONT

IT IS A common error of some critics to say that this or that movie
adaptation is not as good as the novel, short story, or dirty joke
that gave it birth, which is tantamount to saying that Kreisler is a
good musician, but he can't play the violin as well as Liszt could
compose music. As practically all movies are warmed-over best-
sellers of some kind, this criticism finds its way into print every week.
However, it happens that, applied to *All Quiet On the Western
Front*, there is some merit in such a statement. The movie follows
the book, aimlessly but sincerely, and as a result it has little direc-

tion or point. It is a panorama of war, with gunfire, dead men, and all the gruesome paraphernalia. It takes in so much territory and loses itself so often in the trenches that you never do get any feeling of relationship with the hero, who gets himself shot in the end reaching over a trench for a butterfly.

Two of the ablest men in the theatre, Maxwell Anderson and George Abbott, adapted Remarque's simple, calm exposition of war. Unfortunately, either by intent or under orders, they limited their drama by attempting to transpose the novel *in toto* to the screen.

All the characters of the book are vaguely there. But after the first ten minutes the company of boys urged into the trenches by their schoolmaster fades dimly against a background of artillery fire and marching men. There is war for you, but the marching and the dying go nowhere. It is possible that this is the dramatized spirit of the book, but the film gives you none of the strength of the printed word. After all, negation is hard to set afire, and I know of no method for symbolizing indifference.

For ten minutes *All Quiet On the Western Front* is alive and active. The enthusiastic schoolboys go to war as though it were a football training camp. The Anderson dialogue crackles like the vivid words of his *What Price Glory*. Until these lads reach the front, everything, from the sets with mist rising off the front of a dawn to the schoolboy's naïve introduction to shellfire, molds into a lifelike real story. But when the director sets his characters in the trenches, this unity disintegrates. There are long, meaningless speeches by the hero, there are shots of men going over the top, time after time, that are over-long, monotonous. Certainly here is a picture of war, but it is a pageant, not a drama, of war.

If the producers had told Mr. Anderson and Mr. Abbott to go out and sit over a teacup and write a war play, there is little doubt but that they would have turned out a good job. As it is, they have done handsomely by a novel that from a reading shows little or no possibilities for the limited area of the screen. In the novel, you have a full-grown man telling you how he grew old, surrounded by the corpses of his friends. On the screen, you have a none-too-competent youth talking about how old he feels. The very melancholy beat of the words in the novel drum like a funeral roll. There are so many detached scenes, so many repetitious tragedies in the movie, the death of the hero comes as an anti-climax. It certainly came as no shock.

It is possible that a real actor might have put power in *All Quiet On the Western Front*. The one scene Lew Ayres had with Beryl Mercer was proof enough of his inexperience. She alone seemed real, and by her sure treatment of the few banal lines given her, she had the audience reaching for its handkerchiefs and mumbling under its breath.

I wish it had been a better movie. There is no doubt that it will be successful, but if two writers and a director of the caliber responsible for *All Quiet On the Western Front* had been allowed money and opportunity to produce an original work, the result would have been far more exciting. What they have done has power, but it is spread all over the place. If no one had ever read a novel with the incidents put on the screen, this expressive feature would be hailed as something far short of a masterpiece, and even a movie producer would be able to see that *The Case of Sergeant Grischa* and, emphatically, *Journey's End* came nearer putting life and war on the screen.

Judge, May 24, 1930

OLD AND NEW

WITH interviews, lecture engagements, and luncheons, the Russian movie director, Sergei Eisenstein, is being welcomed to the country. Mr. Eisenstein has been loaned by the Soviet government to that old radical group, Paramount, and he had hardly set foot on our Republican soil before he was snapped up for banquets and speeches and toured around the town in Rolls Royces by the local proletariat. The Amtorg Trading Company, the Amkino Movie Company, and even their government may be suffering under the delusion that this sudden dancing in the street over Russian art is merely a prelude to a local revolution, but if they have followed our enthusiasms during the post-war period they may discover that we have passed rapidly from Mah-Jongg and the promotion of Negro art into a Soviet trance without danger to the Republican party, and Mr. Eisenstein would do well to sell short while the market is high.

While I do not share the local opinion that Eisenstein is the messiah of the infant industry, his work has been so little distributed over the country it deserves praise. His latest production, *Old and New*, is by far the best thing he has done. It is admittedly propaganda, a lecture to the slow-witted habitants of the steppes on the blessings of cooperative farming. Eisenstein makes it as palatable as possible by grouping faces and figures against setting suns and decayed hovels, and it is this knack of design and photography that has brought him deserved fame. His method is simple: his characters are used as dummies, pigments in his color scheme. However, Murnau used practically the same method in *Sunrise*; and Chaplin, with old-fashioned equipment, was seeking this effect in *A Woman of Paris*. If the best directors in Hollywood were given *carte blanche*, allowed to pick their cast from the population of the entire country as the Soviet allows its Number One director, there is little doubt that Lubitsch, Vidor, and a half-dozen others could give the Russians real competition at their own game.

While Eisenstein does not possess a startling new technique, the present Russian hysteria has so affected the producers they will let him work unhindered on the Gold Coast, and whatever he does will be worth seeing. To me, the sight of hundreds of International Harvesters turned over to millions of farmers producing crops cooperatively was more significant than the beautiful designs of Eisenstein, and if you want a good tip on the next war to end competition, try to see *Old and New*.

Judge, June 21, 1930

PASTRY; ROXY'S USHERS

THERE IS every reason to believe that within a year movies will not be of the same monotonous form and character. At the present time, the large companies have succeeded in producing their movies with rigid constructions. The actual form, the technique of the film, has no more variation from day to day than a Ford chassis. Occasionally, some daring producer will tack on a cigar lighter, a new coat of paint, or an extra tire, but the form of the movie has, with a few rare exceptions, remained static ever since Hollywood began its great era of sound. Strangely enough, even the public seems to have felt the monotony, despite the theory that nothing is too terrible for a movie fan.

Whatever the reason, the great corporations have discovered suddenly that the gold is not cascading into the cashier's drawer as it once did. Warner Brothers withheld its quarterly dividend last week, and before the year is out the Brothers will have plenty of anxious company. The Guaranty Trust Company has issued a report on the infant industry, characterizing it as a mushroom growth, unsound and risky. All of which is no news to the producers. But it may bring home to the gentlemen once again that, despite the opinion of the Supreme Court, which held that the movies were "concerned with industry—not with art, news or opinion," even the most loyal movie fan needs some meat along with his cheap pastry.

Roxy has turned his ushers into spies, just as I anticipated the day he hired a Marine to drill them. Every half-hour one of these grim young men tiptoes up to a customer and listens to his or her comment on the film. While this is supposed to be a perfectly fair system, I am not too certain that everything is aboveboard, and I would not be surprised to hear soon that any customer found grumbling, biting fingernails, hissing, or otherwise disparaging the attempts of the master, may be put on a blacklist and eventually find the golden doors of the cathedral closed against him. After all, there is enough precedent for such a system. There are bogus convicts in our Federal prisons, half the bootleggers one meets are undercover men, and I know a number of astute fellows who still don't believe that the census was all that it was supposed to be. Personally, I haven't been able to get into Roxy's in months. His outer ushers look like circus giants and they so clutter up the entrance that it is an afternoon's job to get through the ranks, much less elicit any information from them. If any of you are interested, I would be delighted to institute a counter-organization against Roxy's. Covered with false whiskers and badges, we might sneak up to the customers and plant little acorns of discontent in their ears. It might not be fair, but it would be fun.

Judge, August 30, 1930

HELL'S ANGELS

THE MOVIE epic of the season is *Hell's Angels*. It is not great, but it is as lavish as an eight-ring circus, and when you leave the theatre you will know you have seen a movie and not a tinny reproduction of a stage show. The movie is too long, there is one color scene that never should have been done, the story is given over to an uncomprehending, mediocre actor, and there is one horrific mawkish line in the concluding scene. Yet *Hell's Angels* has power and you need not remember that there was a story or a leading man. You will remember a Zeppelin nosing through a white cloud, making London cower in darkness. You will remember a power dive through the cloudy sky, and you will not soon forget the sheer beauty of the aerial fight portrayed against a floor of fascinating cloud formations.

While the story is not important, young Joseph Moncure March has achieved some distinction when you consider the sniveling sentiment of the home brand war scenarios furnished by Hollywood in the past. His noble young man never seems important, a responsibility James Hall, an undistinguished movie actor, shares with the author. Not even Mr. March seemed to believe very much in this hero, who shoots his brother in order to preserve the honor of the family. But there is a good-humored, bawdy atmosphere in many of the scenes, and Ben Lyon and a buxom young lady by the name of Jean Harlow put unusual gusto into their work. A great many things will be cut by the censors in Pennsylvania and Ohio, but if the scene in which Miss Harlow appears in what might have been an evening gown before it was left out in the rain, and then so innocently asks, "Do you mind if I change into something more comfortable?" is censored, drop me a note and I'll gladly describe the scene in as much detail as the editor will allow.

Much of the dialogue is in German, an unnecessary striving for realism that slows the action. The pre-war scenes are slow and relieved only by the very healthy Miss Harlow. The cameraman and the crew of commercial fliers who yank their ships up and down beautiful skies are the real heroes of *Hell's Angels*, and their work furnishes a good evening's entertainment.

Judge, September 6, 1930

WHERE ARE THE SET DESIGNERS?

JUST before the movies entered into their garrulous old age, the Germans were setting the styles in Hollywood. Camera angles became a fetish, and you seldom got a good look at the figures or faces of the characters—one foot, a hip, or a tooth would be shot carelessly around the corner at you. The German school not only established this set of tricks, but they brought their own furniture into prominence. Leni's *The Man Who Laughs* was one of the best and most interesting of the last batch of silent films. His outdoor sets were very good, but his modernistic designs of a gallows and of a circus were exceptionally effective; the producers, as is their custom, figured if a futuristic set helped a Victor Hugo scenario it necessarily would appreciate the value of all epics. Thus *Broadway* came out in movie form with a café that was twice the size of Grand Central Station and as foreign to a Broadway night-club as pre-war whisky. For about six months the producers used these futuristic sets for every movie they made, creating an atmospheric background of a drug addict on the loose in a Crane bathroom factory.

Then came the talkies (and now I'm sneaking up on an idea); sound engineers, dialogue directors, and an entirely new set of virtuosos moved into the Gold Coast factories. Unfortunately, nobody thought it necessary to hire scenic designers. Today there is only one designer in Hollywood who really builds beautiful sets: William Cameron Menzies, designer to Fairbanks these many years.

There are several distinguished workmen in the theatre: Bel-Geddes, Jones, Reynolds, Throckmorton. Not one has been sent to Hollywood, although all the assistant assistant directors in the world are on salary in the movie factories. Until the directors rebel, we shall have to take our movies surrounded with the bathroom architecture left by the departed Teutons.

Judge, September 13, 1930

Peroration No. 2
MORAL RACKETEERING IN THE MOVIES

M OVIE censorship receives almost as much notice in the press as the mundane habits of movie stars. Bulls from the office of Will Hays and statements from the various uplift leagues give one the impression that censorship breaks out over the industry like the measles and disappears as rapidly. As a matter of fact, there is a well-organized and stable machinery set up to smooth and purify all the celluloid that appears in the land, whether manufactured in Hollywood or abroad—and to protect the dividends resulting therefrom.

This machinery is composed of three elements: (1) six sets of minor politicians in as many states; (2) Will Hays, ex-Postmaster-General in the Cabinet of Warren G. Harding, created "czar" of the nation's third largest industry by grace of the Fatty Arbuckle scandal; (3) the National Board of Review. The last two are results of what might well be termed "moral racketeering."

Circumstances have allowed this machine to work undercover. Mr. Hays, as the super press agent of the industry, could not be expected to present a factual picture of movie censorship or of the real purpose of his organization. The most powerful censors are appointed by governors, and it would be optimistic indeed to expect a politician voluntarily to betray the mysterious workings of his office. The women's clubs, which are to a large extent responsible for both Hays and the National Board of Review, while loquacious enough, have been noted for everything but logic and dignity. But, mysterious as they work, these three groups of censors have combined to mutilate, change, or muddle every movie shown in this country during the past ten years.

Follow a manuscript through the movie factory and you get a clear picture of the activities of undercover agents who exercise an unprecedented right—the right of pre-censorship. Not just one movie goes through this process, but every film you have ever seen.

The play, "Coquette," furnishes an example. It was a fine piece of work—a story of a Southern gentleman of the old school who provoked the death of a boy and girl because they violated the old-school code. The play ran in New York for months and played in many other cities. Critics and audiences gave it unstinted praise. Mary Pickford chose it for her debut in talking pictures. The manuscript was purchased, and George Abbott, co-author and director of the play, was engaged as director. A fine play, a famous player, a good director—you could not ask more of the movies. Work was started. The sales manager held the usual conference with Colonel Joy of the Will Hays office. Miss Pickford was informed that the plot had to be changed; Colonel Joy had conferred with Mrs. Winter (representing the women's clubs in Hollywood) and had come to the conclusion that it would be too much for the general public to have the heroine with child, as the plot demanded. A change was "suggested."

Miss Pickford objected to any change. It was her debut and she did not want to have a crippled plot to work with. The sales manager said it was impossible to expect the state censor boards of Pennsylvania and New York to license the film unless the change was made. The heroine was not to be with child. The father, not the heroine, was to commit suicide. With the entire unity and strength of the play destroyed, they again started to work. But every day Director Abbott received long memorandums from the Hays office. The word "whisky" must not be used—the Kansas censors would object. The heroine must not be kissed on the neck —it was taboo in Maryland. Finally, the movie with its distorted and pointless tragedy was completed. But not yet could the public see it. First it had to be exhibited before five women in New York City. They conferred, marked a ballot, pronounced the work good, and a seal, "Passed by the National Board of Review," was attached to the film. The battered print was then presented to six state censor boards. Each state demanded a few changes (no two boards agreeing on a change). There were more conferences with the sales manager. And finally *Coquette* was presented to the public. In Cleveland or any other city, Miss Helen Hayes could perform the play as originally written before any group of people without one voice being lifted in protest. Around the corner in a movie theatre, Mary Pickford had to present a vitiated version of the same play—vitiated by no wish of the movie customers.

The producers of *Coquette* did not override Miss Pickford and accept the demands of the women's clubs for the sake of sweet chivalry, nor did they agree to the demands of the state boards out of politeness.

If every motion picture theatre prefaced its films with the caption, "This picture has been censored by a minor politician or his assistants," the patrons might be made to understand why the movies are so banal and childish.

It is the six state boards of censors that wield the principal power in the film-censorship machine. These boards exist in New York, Pennsylvania, Maryland, Virginia, Kansas, and Ohio. The first was created in 1911, the last in 1915. At no time was there a public demand for their existence. When these laws were passed the pants-pressers and furriers who then owned the business were scrambling for patents and theatres. If censorship meant more customers, the producers were for censorship. The movie form was just taking shape. No man realized the potentialities of the industry (Edison sold the British rights to his patents for almost nothing). The producers were too busy to pay any attention to legislatures. As for the public—who cared about the nickelodeon? Yet the censor born in 1911 exists by legislative right, and, as we have discovered so often, it is a hundredfold easier to pass than to repeal a moral law.

A few corporations make forty percent of the world's movies. They also own great theatre chains. The corporations dance to the tune the censors play for the simple reason that the censors have the power by law to demand changes that will cost thousands of dollars. Under the present circumstances, a movie clipped in Pennsylvania is usually shipped on to several states so that the citizens of Kentucky, West Virginia, and North Carolina are forced to accept Pennsylvania's censored version of art.

It is hardly necessary to point out that three people with young girls or old women for assistants could hardly expect to maintain good judgment after sitting nine hours a day watching movies for signs of evil-doing. So many movies are produced the boards admit they cannot do justice to their work. The chairman of the New York board, in asking for help, told the legislature it was necessary at the present time to employ state troopers to help the board.

Yet no matter how careful a producer may be, the state censor must cut something, else how would he keep his job? The Virginia chairman actually prefaced his yearly report with the headline, "Business Better Than Ever!" and then went on to boast of the great number of cuts his board made last year.

The head of the Maryland board is a druggist-doctor-politician. He has run for various offices at several times as the candidate of a Wet party. Contrast him with the head of the Kansas board, Miss Emma Viets. She received her education running a movie theatre in Girard, Kansas. She has never allowed one drinking scene or any use of the word "whisky" to titillate the fancy of Kansas moviegoers. The director has to steer between the two schools of politicial thought—the customer gets the benefit.

A majority of the changes the censors demand are ridiculous. All of them are tyrannous and questionable. *The Patriot* and *The Racket* furnish two examples. Many people claim that *The Patriot* was the greatest film ever made in this country. Certainly it was a superior piece of work. It was written by Alfred Neumann, the German playwright, and presented on the stage in New York. It came out in book form and was not manhandled even by John Sumner and his crew. Lubitsch, one of the best directors in the world, selected this play for his fellow-countryman, Emil Jannings.

From the sets to the tempo, here was a movie that showed skill, that offered entertainment far beyond the usual childish romance of the screen. Not one box-office compromise was made. The play was not altered by one word. It has been accepted on two continents as a worthy piece of literature. What was the result? The censors of Pennsylvania filled three paragraphs with instructions for changes. They eliminated practically every scene between Jannings, as the mad Paul II, and Florence Vidor, merely because Jannings was making childlike, pathetic love to his friend's mistress. If these scenes were pornographic, then no movie could be shown in Pennsylvania. But you could not expect much discrimination from three politicians of a commonwealth that boasts of the Vare machine. *The Patriot* was changed by each of the six state boards, but Pennsylvania did the most damage.

The Racket explains a new and significant censor-fear. This play was written by a Chicago newspaper man. In Hemingway dialogue, it told the story of an honest police captain struggling against the enormously corrupt machinery of his city and state. As a stage play, it was successful and ran unmolested in New York City. The state movie censors of New York eliminated every scene and all titles that even suggested graft. Not only that, but both the Pennsylvania and New York censors cut a scene in which a young policeman taunts a gangster and is shot in the back for his courage. It is significant that no other censor board saw harm in this scene. Graft and crime now worry these two boards as much as sex; in fact, fifty percent of the cuts made last year came under the heading, "Inciting to crime."

Religion, politics, and marital relations are cut to the most banal situations. Little of Ibsen, Shakespeare, O'Neill, or Tolstoy could reach the screen in original form. The three Tolstoy manuscripts that have been filmed are almost unrecognizable. The Pennsylvania board actually forced the producers to make an entire scene, in the adaptation of *Anna Karenina*, which had Anna married to her lover, a scene that not only was stupid but that destroyed a simple plot that has been read for years by all nations, a story that is required reading in many schools. *Resurrection* was cut in the usual indiscriminate manner, but the producer censored the story in advance—knowing it would not go through—and the heroine according to the movie was just a disappointed girl. There was not much to resurrect. *Redemption*, a recent production, was so mangled it bore absolutely no relation to the play.

The censor boards have seventeen rules of conduct. According to these you cannot:
- portray suicide
- refer to capital punishment
- offend a nation
- offend a religion

- ridicule a politician
- suggest miscegenation
- portray vulgarity
- portray breakdown of justice

There are nine other classifications, equally equivocal, but these alone are enforced in such a manner that the stuff of drama automatically is sheared from the screen. You can mention these subjects only if right—political, neo-Methodist right—succeeds in the end.

I do not think any sane man would choose petty politicians as logical custodians of public morals. It is ridiculous to think of three politicians in each of the six states having legal power to rule a four-billion-dollar business. If a newspaper publisher, a magazine owner, or a theatrical producer were confronted with this onerous group of politicians, he would fight. He would, I am optimistic enough to believe, have at least a minority fighting with him. But your movie corporation exists on a simple mathematical formula of geometrical progression, and one fight would mean the temporary loss of customers and money. While it was fighting in the courts for *Coquette*, a competitor would be filling theatres, increasing dividends. I think the day a producer goes before the people of Pennsylvania with a list of the scenes cut by Censor Knapp and his assistants he can effect a housecleaning. The high pressure of competition secures the board against any such demonstration.

Besides the state censors, the movie goes through two other purifying rooms: Hays and his clubwomen delegates and the National Board of Review. Will Hays has created, for public consumption, a mythological figure of himself clothed in robes of chastity. He receives a quarter of a million dollars or more from the major movie companies for his work, and he is indisputably the key man of the industry. He is not hired, however, because of a peculiar ability to determine the pure from the pornographic. Since he was nineteen, he has been a politician. He became interested in the movies while managing Harding's campaign. He had seen to it that the late President got his amiable countenance in several miles of film. When the Fatty Arbuckle case brought a tigress cry from every women's club in the country, the nervous producers called Hays into conference, made him czar. Immediately he laid down a barrage of propaganda which he continues to this day. He saw to it that no action was taken in Washington, and he played ball with the women's clubs and the churches.

The women gave Will Hays his job, and he has fostered their strength until today he allows twelve delegates from women's clubs to confer with his agent, Colonel Joy, while movies are actually in production. Some of these women claim to be only personal delegates, others claim to represent millions of mothers. Whatever they represent, you have twelve ladies sending neat reports to Colonel Joy each day on the progress of our national art, you have the National Board of Review given the privilege of "commenting" on films before public presentation. He also allows the companies under his care to pay the National Board of Review for putting their seal of approval on every film out of Hollywood. The twelve delegates have no legal authority, the board has none, Mr. Hays has none—yet the movies follow their "suggestions"!

The clubwomen, headed by Mrs. Winter, former president of the General Federation of Women's Clubs, are allowed to read all books and novels considered for production by the Hays companies (and they are the only important units in the business). The producers do not readily agree with the demands of the ladies, but they have to humor them. All the girls were against a filming of *The Green Hat* after a second reading. Mr. Hays passed along the word, but MGM merely changed the title and the hero's disease and *A Woman of Affairs* was made. Maryland and Virginia censored the major love scene, but the women didn't burn this bit of heresy.

The D.A.R. urgently protested "An American Tragedy" and it was not filmed, although a producer gave Dreiser $90,000 for the right to do so, and production was stopped merely because the director made twelve reels from the first chapter.

Mr. Hays's suave staff of assistants coddles the ladies into uselessness in many instances. But a riot would ensue should "Strange Interlude," "Revelry," or any other controversial play reach the screen. So long as the producers allow Mr. Hays to entertain the clubwomen, the movies cannot go far beyond the understanding of the Ladies' Aid.

The story of the National Board of Review is typical of Anglo-Saxon censorship. In 1909, Mayor McClellan of New York City closed down the new nickelodeons as a political gesture. The head of the People's Institute, one of the most admirable public institutions in the country, offered to form a board to review films and suggest to the producers their merits or faults. At that time he made a flat statement that "the People's Institute is against censorship of any kind." He also suggested to the mayor that there were several things in New York City more deadly than the struggling nickelodeons.

Today the National Board of Review makes a weak attempt to follow the original founder's creed. It does recommend "better films." It does issue a list of pictures suitable for children. It does attempt to point out to its national chapters the artistic merit of our best films. It does claim that it is not a censorship organization. Against these admirable habits is the fact that in return for its "suggestions" the National Board is paid by the foot by the movie producers. It is not that Will Hays is not capable of control. It is that the National Board of Review has local chapters in most cities in the country and, as a member of the Hays office said, "It is better to have all the women in one place so you know what they are squawking about."

In other words, the National Board of Review is paid by the movies for the same reason that Chicago laundrymen pay gangsters: protection.

The board objects to this statement. But five people must have salaries (the executive staff), office expenses must be paid—they cannot get enough money by contributions to keep going, so the movies pay them. Naturally, the movies are not paying any organization for fun, are not giving them the privilege of pre-inspection for nothing. The board can, and says it can, arouse local chapters, correspond with women's clubs, agitate an Arbuckle storm again if it so desires.

The actual workers of the National Board are as mysterious as the state censors. The most important branch of the organization is the "reviewing committee." This committee is chosen each week from a list of two hundred and fifty women who work without pay. Who are they? Middle-aged women from the suburbs and outskirts of New York City who have nothing else to do. They have a ballot which they mark. This ballot is probably one of the most miraculous documents ever connected with an art. Can you imagine a board of nondescript women marking the works of Oscar Wilde, Fielding, Hemingway, Shakespeare even, rating them "Good," "Educational," "Subversive to morality"?

The board, if it could exist independently, might be put to admirable use. At present it is tied. Whether it likes it or not, it is a censorship organization. Florida has a statute to the effect that only films accepted by the National Board of Review may be shown in that state. There is a mayor's order in Boston to the same effect. Thus, if the board would refuse to put its seal on a film, that picture could not be shown in Florida. Five women in New York dictate to the entire movie audience of Florida. That smells somewhat of censorship.

A great many earnest people are interested in the National Board of Review: teachers, doctors, lawyers. They do little reviewing—that is left to the volunteer women. The board has consistently gone on record against legal censorship. But what good can they do, how much can they fight? A recent campaign is a fair example. An English producer sent a film called *High Treason* to New York. The board passed it, recommended it to their national chapters. The state censors of New York and Pennsylvania banned the picture, refused to let it be shown anywhere in either state, although it is now being shown elsewhere in the country.

High Treason was shown privately by the National Board before a group of writers, artists, and lawyers. It was a sound, imaginative drama of the next war. The dramatic interest was between the leader of a peace army and the president of the Federated European States. The peace-army leader assassinates the president in order to prevent war, and is then sentenced to death by an English court. Outside of its admirable futuristic camera effects, the movie is a harmless bit of peace propaganda. The two state censor boards refused to give any reason for their ban.

After the private showing sponsored by the National Board, two prominent criminal lawyers volunteered their services. They said they would fight the two state censor boards and make them show cause for their action. They volunteered to solicit money and inform the movie patrons of the two states of the merits of the condemned film. The National Board executives refused this legal aid. They said: "The English producer who owns the film does not want a fight. If he angers the Hays office, where will he show his pictures in the future?"

"Then," the executives were asked, "is the Hays office actually in favor of state censorship?"

"When it bans foreign competitors it is," was the answer.

The lawyers still wanted to fight. They asked the National Board why its position with its local chapters would be hurt by a fight for a private movie company any more than the fact that it accepts money from Hollywood endangers its position. The answer is obvious. So long as the National Board of Review has to take money from the Hollywood companies it cannot afford to fight the policies of Will Hays. And, it would seem, the state censors can afford to do this bit for Mr. Hays's group of American producers in return for the jobs which the industry has created for them.

Never has an art form been subjected to such control. If tomorrow you were to organize a company and make a movie, what could you do with it? You would need a theatre. All the urban movie theatres are owned or controlled by the big movie corporations. Suppose you hired a small independent theatre. In six states, the censors have the power to forbid absolutely the appearance of your work; a volunteer group of women demands the right to pass on your work before the public has a chance to praise or condemn it. How can a foreign producer present his work to the public unless he joins the Hays organization, unless he grants every demand of the theatre owners, who happen to be competing producers? There is no way out. Free speech, opinion, art—such words fade into the dim record of another day when you approach the movie industry. It is ruled by fear and is a victim of moral racketeering.

The movie may be a legitimate art form. The best technicians in the world are in Hollywood, and they have achieved beauty in form many times, but the content of their art remains childish. To battle the censors, the women, a super-politician, and a dividend-cautious producer is too much to ask of any artist. It is no wonder that a trip to Hollywood is regarded by writers as a descent into hell, a free ride to a psychopathic ward, a fantastic dream of wealth without content. And it is easy to understand why a so-called art that has risen to be a world industry monotonously produces vacuous, cheap, and banal entertainment.

Scribner's, September, 1930

LAUGHTER

I CANNOT understand why two such droll and deft fellows as Donald Ogden Stewart and Henry D'Ababbie D'Arrast should have felt it necessary to spread a thin smear of theatrical paste over a very skillful piece of work. *Laughter*, without its pointed title, is a swift satirical piece marked at intervals by superb dialogue and the quick hand of a smart director. It is marred by the periodic cackles of a talented cast who had to support the foolish title by emphasizing each peroration of the plot with a laugh, in order, I presume, to get it over to the ladies' culture clubs, the church drama leagues, and Will Hays.

Director D'Arrast did not let his laughs become offensive and, outside of a bewilderment as to why he ever let such a phony idea loose anyway, I couldn't complain heavily at its inclusion, because he has turned out a talkie with so fast a pace that it crowds the comprehension of half the movie customers, a fact which will not cause me to toss sleeplessly in my bed for many nights.

I have never seen better acting in the movies than the show put on by Frank Morgan, Fredric March, Glenn Anders, and Diane Ellis. Unfortunately for Nancy Carroll, the aforementioned young lady and the three gentlemen, under the impetus of good dialogue and one of the few cultivated directors in the business, completely outweigh her. Miss Carroll, as a result of a sound piece of work in *The Devil's Holiday*, was hailed by a few thousand syndicated columns as a Bernhardt, and all the shouting went to the head of Paramount's sales department. She is starred in *Laughter* and she is incompetent, not because of complete inadequacy but because of competition. Mr. Morgan is one of those handy men who can take pratfalls in a musical comedy one night and do a creditable Hamlet the next, and I suggest that Miss Carroll take a look at the scenes in which Morgan is supposed to be a Wall Street Babbitt; by neat side-stepping he fooled Mr. Stewart and became a very sympathetic and important man and, in fact, stole the movie right from under Mr. D'Arrast's camera.

Fredric March, as a nervous young musician stepping lightly out of society's bounds, is fortunate in that he was awarded the best—and I think they are the best he has yet written—of Mr. Stewart's comedy lines.

And right here I want to make a little speech of thanks to Mr. Stewart for giving me an opportunity to make my contribution to the theory of the drama for 1930–1931. As long as I can remember, plays or movies that have what is supposed to be a crowd of gay dogs in it include a scene in which the boys and girls sit in a circle and reminisce about the funny things that happened in the past. The boys and girls then laugh hollowly (as well they might, because invariably the things that happened are not such as would appeal to an actor as being fun) and the customer immediately gets suspicious. Personally, I always get antagonistic towards the author at this point and think of some of the times I have had, and how much funnier the things I did were than the tame parties the boys and girls describe. Therefore, Mr. Stewart, it is neither funny nor effective to talk about old times on the stage, and I hope I get a star on my report card for having been such a bright boy.

Mr. Stewart has been fortunate, or else very exacting, with movie producers. This is the second time a manuscript of his has had the phenomenal good fortune of finding itself in the hands of a director possessing skill and good taste. *Laughter* deals with a chorus girl who throws over an artist and a musician to marry a banker. Miss Carroll has played opposite Mr. Charles (Buddy) Rogers too often to stand up against the ability of Mr. Morgan and Miss Ellis. She not only does not act like a chorus girl, she doesn't act like a banker's wife, which seemed to be her intention.

However, from Greenwich Village to Greenwich, D'Arrast has given extraordinarily effective pictures of New York, and they are so deft it makes little difference at times whether the chorus girl shoots the artist or whether he shoots himself, which, as a matter of fact, is what he does. In conclusion, I congratulate Paramount on the subtle cunning of their production staff. They hired a movie director, and not a stage director, and one of the best in the business; they gave him a manuscript by a more-than-competent writer, and they allowed him to hire, with one exception, a proved cast.

As a further note on the success of this policy, I point to the proof that when George Kaufman and Ring Lardner write a play, and a producer hires a good cast, more than often the result is a good show. I go to all this trouble because I think this theory is too seldom observed by the producers. Now that they have seen it work, they might try it again.

Judge, December 6, 1930

SOUS LES TOITS DE PARIS

THE MOST genuine movie I have seen since *Hallelujah* is *Sous les Toits de Paris*. It is a French picture, which only makes the whole thing more amazing. Simple, unaffected, it has a lingering charm that was created by sure-handed direction, excellent lighting, and that indefinable something that manifests itself, even in a movie, when an artist follows through a conception of a worthy job. You do not need to understand French in order to capture the spirit of this simple piece. A boy and a girl are peddling a song on the streets—and a very good song it is, too—and their anxiety is manifested by a quickened tempo. The boy is put in jail—but I do not intend to analyze the many deft touches of direction and pace that make this picture really delightful; that's as silly as defining the mood put on you by a concert devoted entirely to Ravel and Debussy. The leading man, whose name I haven't handy, was easily more engaging than the much-publicized Chevalier, but all credit must go to René Clair, the director. His production is pleasing to the eyes, it is unpretentious, it has the most ingenious direction of any talking picture shown in this country and, furthermore, all this comes out of a nation that long has been noted for its atrocious movies. Which makes Monsieur Clair head director of the business as far as I'm concerned.

Judge, January 24, 1931

CITY LIGHTS

CHARLES SPENCER CHAPLIN's new movie, *City Lights*, does not prove any of the hundred-and-one things some of the boys have been claiming for it these past few years, but I don't see just why it should. It has some very funny scenes in it, and they more than compensate for the price of admission.

In a way it is fortunate that *City Lights* is supposed to be a "defiance hurled at the talkies," otherwise I should have very little to write about. I'm not conscience-stricken at the idea of wasting your time and annoying the copyreaders with a description of the number of times Mr. Chaplin falls into a lake, pulling a drunk with him, or of the magnificent sense of timing which makes the prize-fight dance a side-splitting affair, but since the boys have given me so many leads I might as well forego this form of idiocy for another and roll up my sleeves and discuss drama, and the fragile tragedy that hangs gently over the work of Mr. Chaplin.

As you may have learned from United Press, International News, Associated Press, and five hundred thousand columns, *City Lights* is a picture without dialogue. It is not as ambitious as some of the earlier Chaplin comedies, and technically is almost old-fashioned—evidently the master has not seen many movies these last three years—but if you ever liked Chaplin, you will find that he has done all his old tricks over again, carefully and painstakingly, and they were funnier than ever to me. Unfortunately, Chaplin has underscored the ancient aria from "Pagliacci" heavier than ever, and but for a naked exhibition of the man's ego at the end of the show—a close-up that you will not soon forget—the picture would have been downright messy.

Even though Mr. Woollcott and Mr. Seldes may have convinced the famous comedian that he is a world force; despite the fact that William Lyons Phelps probably will discover that heartbreaking little Charlot is a symbol of the spiritual urge in a machine age; even though the artist may have tried to echo all this significance—I still can see no reason why *City Lights* should be treated with all the solemn pomp of a christening in a corporation laboratory.

From a business standpoint, Chaplin would have been silly if he had made a talking picture. Harpo Marx drew a good salary for saying nothing, and because some unfortunate mechanic learned how to photograph sound waves is no logical reason for Mr. Marx to change his style of entertainment. *City Lights* offers nothing new in the way of direction, lighting, or musical accompaniment—*Sous les Toits de Paris* shows infinitely more imaginative direction. It proves nothing, except that Mr. Chaplin is the greatest clown we have, and that's enough. Personally, I don't need sets by Urban and lighting by Ziegfeld to laugh my head off at W. C. Fields when he tries patiently to rid himself of a few sheets of tissue paper.

I do take exception to the old joke about the drunk and the car in *City Lights*—Chaplin's gagmen cheated him on that one—and I believe that the slowest movie audience will find the pace of the sentimental scenes boring and unnecessary. For all of these things, *City Lights* is a damned sight funnier than the combined works of Amos 'n Andy plus all the talking comedies produced since 1928.

Up to this point, I have been utterly selfish in enjoying my own superior understanding of the season's most important production. I hope no fanatic tears this sheet from our family journal, prints extra copies and hands them out on street corners, because I earnestly believe that nothing would be more beneficial to the health of the body politic than a hue and cry from the masses for silent pictures. I hope the boys can prove to every art patron, drama lover, and ladies' aid secretary in the land that *City Lights* is the most ingenious work of art ever devised by man and that it proves conclusively talking pictures are through.

For three years, directors and producers have tried to think of something to do with their expensive electrical equipment. How glorious if Mr. Chaplin's world-wide audience should rise as one man and say "Throw it away!" We then would be right back where we started, according to the Lewis theory; instead of Gary Cooper we would have Tom Mix; and instead of Hoover, the Northampton Oracle. Believe me, I would be willing to plug *City*

Lights as a world force for all I'm worth if by so doing we could achieve another industrial revolution.

And while I feel so genial, I want to congratulate Mr. Chaplin's representatives for the manner in which they handled the opening of his show. It was easy to get into the theatre and once in, there were no hoodlums in ermine and evening clothes to put on a Hollywood demonstration. Such a first night was a much more amazing phenomenon to me than anything that was presented in the movie itself.

Judge, February 28, 1931

DISHONORED

I HAVE not yet become excited over Marlene (Legs) Dietrich to the extent of writing, or reading, pieces explaining why she personifies Mysterious Womanhood, but for at least the third time the gentleman who directs her movies has shown himself an unusual and gifted cameraman. Joseph Sternberg cannot get near a movie camera without doing things that prove him a man with a real and original understanding of the power of the motion picture camera. Yet—and I hope some of the great minds pay some attention to my profound advice—the Messrs. Wanger, Lasky, and their assistants, who furnish Mr. Sternberg celluloid, should make every effort in the future to keep him away from a typewriter. *Dishonored* is the most exciting movie that I have seen in several months, yet I hope I may die young if I ever have to listen to a manuscript so full of recusant, stilted, outmoded theatrical mouthings as you find in this one—and Mr. Sternberg helped write it. I have mentioned this before. *The Case of Lena Smith* was a display of camera sense, *Street of Sin* was a Billy Sunday lecture, illustrated by Herr Jannings, *The Salvation Hunters* was a first effort at impressionistic direction and had not even the beginning of a story to it. These things Mr. Sternberg either wrote or helped to write. A Mr. Hecht wrote *Underworld* and, thanks to a story that was almost perfect, Sternberg did his best work. But keep him away from that typewriter!

Offhand, I cannot list the number of times *Dishonored* has been written for magazine, book, and stage. It is the story of a lady who is engaged to spy for her country and, being only a woman, she falls in love with the second man she has to meet in the line of duty. She saves the man from death and is executed for her fidelity. Starting with this complete outline, the dialogue writers used *East Lynne* as a model of dramaturgy and actually put on paper words that even in these talkie days seldom have been seriously employed as dramatic sentences. Yet, notwithstanding this almost completely idiotic handicap, *Dishonored* is pretty exciting.

You may think it is because of the aforementioned Marlene (Legs) Dietrich, but I assure you—at the risk of being recommended to Freud or worse—that the charm, lure, or ability of the lady have little or nothing to do with the excitement of the show. As he did Pauline Starke and Esther Ralston, Sternberg dramatizes Miss Dietrich with lights and music until, if she were a semi-invalid, she nevertheless would appear exotic and powerful. No man has yet used music as successfully in both silent and sound pictures as this fellow. He has Miss Dietrich playing a Chopin étude, I believe, while he monkeys around framing her face in lights, sneaking behind the piano and getting close-ups of her hair and her figure, projecting her emotion with every device possible to picture and sound. If, with that aid, she didn't appear interesting, she would be a monstrosity. I do not mean to diminish the abilities of Miss Dietrich, but I do insist that as long as she has such a director it is not necessary—or possible either, I suspect—for her to do anything but follow directions and be grateful for her good fortune.

I would like to talk more about Sternberg's use of music, but I will be kind and merely advise you to see *Dishonored* and forget the much-publicized Miss Dietrich and watch the very unusual lights and sets with which she is photographed—and make a mental check on the number of times good music replaces revolting dialogue.

Judge, March 28, 1931

FRONT PAGE

WITH NO regard whatsoever for the ladies' clubs, the children's aid societies, or the censors and Will Hays, Howard Hughes has made the most rip-roaring movie that ever came out of Hollywood. "Front Page" was a hilariously bawdy play with shotgun dialogue, but that is not important; movies have been made from plays before, but seldom have they retained such raucous humor as that supplied by Ben Hecht and Charles MacArthur. *Front Page*, regardless of its antecedents, is an extraordinary movie, and I advise you to see it before Mr. Hays, Mr. Akerson or the Republican Committee on Humor burn all the available prints.

The action of the movie takes place in Chicago's City Hall press room. It is the eve of a hanging and the gentlemen of the press are waiting to report the hanging to their various newspapers. Their conversations, their monologues over telephones come under the head of the bawdiest, funniest words ever issued from all the 22,-000 screens in the nation's movie palaces. There is a plot concerning a reporter who is trying to leave the business, marry, and live respectably, and there is a villain in the form of a city editor who works to prevent his escape, but the plot is not important. The blatant, case-hardened, irreverent dialogue of the police reporters is gorgeously funny and it is this dialogue that makes *Front Page* an extraordinary movie.

Before I go any further I want to call attention to a young man named Howard Hughes. It is not important that he is young or that he earns some thousands of dollars every tick of the clock from some oil property; it is worth noticing that he has produced four of the best movies in the history of Hollywood. They are *Two Arabian Knights, The Racket, Hell's Angels*, and *Front Page*. He hired two young men to make two of these, and very able young men they are. Bartlett Cormack wrote *The Racket* and I liked it. Mr. Cormack was hired by Hughes to adapt his play and Lewis Milestone directed it. *The Racket* was a forthright, unpretentious, gratifying production. Mr. Cormack has adapted *Front Page* and

Milestone handles the camera. It is the best job Hughes has produced.

The movie has faults. Adolphe Menjou is almost too light and airy to effectively present the character of a noted Chicago editor. There are times when he engages in fatuous self-gratification, but in the concluding and fast-moving scenes of the show he is excellent. Mr. Menjou was a last-minute selection for the part, I have been told, because of the death of Louis Wolheim, and considering the fact that Menjou has had little opportunity in talking movies, he did a very good job. What should've been the great scene of the movie does not come off because Cormack either was ordered or felt it necessary to rewrite the scene wherein a prostitute commits suicide. Originally in the second act curtain scene, the girl commits suicide just as Burns, the city editor, walks into the room. As changed for the movie, the girl has a sentimental, over-long dialogue with a murderer and instead of jumping she falls accidentally to her death. The sentimental scene makes her death and the editor's uproarious comment to the murderer anticlimactical and unfunny. On the other hand, Cormack has added to the play a short sequence in which the murderer is being examined by an alienist, and it had me rolling and groaning in the aisle, and for that I'm not going to complain about the sentimental addition to the show.

The gentleman who played the sheriff was guilty of atrocious over-acting, as was the ham who played the mayor. On the other hand, Messrs. Moore, Catlett, Horton, and Summerville were far better than I have ever seen them, and Pat O'Brien, new to Hollywood, gave a performance that must have been almost a perfect re-creation of the character created by the authors, so I can't score much against casting and performances.

Director Milestone has done wonders with the camera and uses it much more concisely and accurately than he did with *All Quiet On the Western Front*. His portraiture of each reporter speeds the action of the dialogue; there are some beautiful snapshots of the prison yard, of the City Hall corridors, yet he holds the shots down to bare necessity. His timing is almost perfect, because the audience I sat with tore the rafters down laughing, yet didn't miss a single line. Milestone has always shown originality, but this time he has an unusual ease and facility with the camera and you seldom get the static, stilted condition so prevalent in talking movies.

Chief credit for *Front Page* should go, of course, to Ben Hecht and Charles MacArthur for writing the thing. However, I am not supposed to be talking about the theatre, and when you consider how many good shows are tortured in Hollywood, *vide June Moon*, etc., etc., and how many shows that are not tortured fail to come off because directors and producers do not see their screen limitations, chief credit for this movie must be given to Howard Hughes, who bought the play and hired smart men to put it on. Hughes is no flash in the pan—as his four productions prove—but above everything else I think he has shown that all the great corporations in the world put together know less about pleasing the public and putting on shows than one mildly intelligent man. I have seen several thousand movies in my day, but I never saw an audience laugh and cheer as it did on this occasion, and even the ushers caught the infection and assumed a sort of to-hell-with-you attitude that was nothing short of shocking.

And it was not because the dialogue was what the ladies will call filthy. Hollywood has put on the filthiest shows in the world merely because the gentlemen producing them do not know the difference between a healthy bawdy joke and a smutty one. Thus they will change a part, such as the songwriter's wife in *June Moon*, and make what might have been hard but amusing, soft but slimy. Some producers contend the public will not stand for it— they ought to watch the public fight to hear *Front Page*. Truth is, a few ministers and old women will not stand for it, and the producers have allowed themselves to be whipped into submission. Personally, there are few movies I could get fighting mad about, but I would appreciate it if any citizen of Pennsylvania, Kansas, Maryland or New York would let me know what Censors Knapp, Viets, Heller and Wingate do with *Front Page*, and if they mangle it I willingly offer to publish the evidence in this column. Here is one movie that is worth a fight.

Judge, April 11, 1931

TABU

A BOUT SEVEN years ago a movie called *The Last Laugh* was shown casually in a few cities. It had been cut by the censors and the last scenes were changed by the director for American audiences, but even with these changes it was a charming and amazingly original motion picture. Four years ago this director was employed by William Fox, and his first Hollywood job was a movie called *Sunrise*. At this time the talkies were just beginning to squawk in the secret recesses of the electricians and had not yet been presented to an incredulous public. *Sunrise*, I am certain, did not issue from Hollywood in the form intended by the director, but, even with a so-called happy ending, I thought at the time, and still believe, that it represented a pure example of the movie form. Not only was it a beautiful thing to see, and not only was it scored with good as well as appropriate music, *Sunrise* was also real and individualistic.

Since 1914, when D. W. Griffith conceived the idea of hiring ten acres of land and ten thousand undraped gals scattered over them to represent "lust," the spectacle picture represented the only real individualistic entertainment in movies. Ordinary movies remained canned burlesque shows or short stories broken up with pictures. *Sunrise* had music, it had a simple story, it needed no captions, and it was as logical and sound a piece of work as a Bach fugue. It was presented in sonata form and built by the director on that structure. *Sunrise* was the work of one man—not a potpourri manufactured by a writer, a sales manager, a shoe clerk, and a pants presser. It was a remarkable achievement.

After *Sunrise*, F. W. Murnau, the director I have been talking about, made one or possibly two movies, but he left Hollywood— always a sign of good taste and intelligence—and went to the South Seas with Robert Flaherty. (I do not know either of the gentlemen, but judging from their work Murnau and Flaherty happened to be two men who had their own ideas about motion pictures and they happened to be two valuable men who could not stand to live and work for long in Hollywood.) Anyway, they went to the South Seas and made a picture called *Tabu*. Murnau directed *Tabu*, but I'm sure Flaherty is responsible for much good work because he was familiar with the area as well as his camera equipment.

Tabu must have pleased Murnau. He was killed several weeks ago in an automobile accident, and I am glad he made such a piece of work before he died. His last picture is far and away his best. Fortunately, he used only native actors, so the producers who are now showing the film could not possibly make new scenes or change even one sequence of the picture. And, even though it has been cut in several states, *Tabu* is as tenuous and lovely as a Debussy concerto. It is silent, but you will not be aware of that. The accompanying musical score is unpretentious but satisfactory. Captions are eliminated by a simple device that does not ever halt continuity. The natives used by Murnau are not only the most beautiful people you will ever see in a movie, but they are so at ease it is hard to believe they actually were aware of the camera. Murnau combined all his skill and conception of the motion picture in this job. A simple story. A beginning, a middle, an end. Scrupulous characterization. And, above all, a charm that usually manifests itself in the work of a good craftsman, even though he uses such an impersonal affair as a camera. *Tabu* is the last job of F. W. Murnau, and it will be remembered as such for a long time.

Judge, April 18, 1931

PUBLIC ENEMY

I LIKE most crime movies because they have real bounce and life in them. Nevertheless, I had decided this week that I had had enough of machine guns and squad cars to last me awhile and that I was not going to like a movie called *Public Enemy*. I was wrong.

Here is another gang picture, but it is a picture with a definite idea and a great deal of sadistic, bloody glee in it, as well as some of the best direction of the year. The two youngsters who wrote this show, Kubec Glasman and John Bright, did away with district attorneys, soft-spoken detectives, and kind-hearted ladies of leisure, and wrote a terse case history of the life and habits of a hoodlum.

Director William Wellman deserves equal praise with the authors for turning out a picture that not only is tougher than any gang show to date but that has a new and excellent angle, the dramatization of the business of crime.

There is no wind-up in *Public Enemy*. A hard-jawed kid is shown boasting about the theft of a pair of roller skates. (His name is not in the program, but he is the only hairy-chested child actor Hollywood has produced to date.) He is excellent. His father, a cop, overhears him, so the kid walks into the house, pauses to unloosen his trouser belt and barks to his stern parent, "How d'ya want 'em this time—up or down?"

From then on, the picture preserves this same idyllic Chicago tempo. After a course in petty thievery that takes him into the post-graduate warehouse class, the hero is hired by bootleggers and before long he develops into a prosperous overbearing killer.

You may think, from this description, that here is another one of those gaudy, wine-women-and-machine-gun romances, but you reckon without Director Wellman. Rather than show a squad of machine-gunners firing away, he lets you hear the whistle of the bullets and the moans of the dying; not pleasant, I'll admit, but effective enough to make you glad you're a bond salesman, a plumber, or even a movie critic, and not a successful bootlegger.

I hope the star of *Public Enemy* gets a chance to do something besides crime movies, but I fear he will be playing one gangster after another because of his work in this production. His name is James Cagney, and while you may not remember him, he has been doing excellent work in the playhouses for several years without excessive praise or reward. He is a good actor.

I have two objections to *Public Enemy*. It is about two hundred feet too long and it has a moral, but I am sure the moral was put there merely to ease the strain on the censors, because there are no sweet young girls, no heroic cops in the show. There is nothing but grim drama.

Judge, May 16, 1931

THE CENSORS

Some months ago several well-known liberals-about-town sat around and discussed censorship, its evils, its precedents, its legality, and the gentlemen who practice it. What seemed so odd to me was that they talked of censors, and people who invoke them, as one would talk about worthy gentlemen, deserving of a fair fight.

I think a look at the things censors do indicates the one unpardonable, infuriating characteristic of the professional censor. When you come right down to it, it is hard to get holier-than-thou toward a family man who has worked for his political party and who supports three or four grown children by serving as an appointed censor. The system is wrong, of course, and the public should change the system and all that, but if the man held his job as easily and tolerantly as an ordinary healthy patrolman who doesn't go around arresting every petty offender on his beat (he'd have the jails full if he did), if he regarded it as a means of support and not as a means of entrance into the pearly gates, you couldn't honestly regard him as a worm.

But I have read censors' cuts and I have heard them talk and sex, crime, immorality, and espionage actually do not interest them so much as fun. For instance, in *Public Enemy* a hoodlum shoves a grapefruit into the face of his girl friend. Admittedly, it is not a pleasant custom, nor one practiced in the best of families. However, the scene was consistent with the character, it was not immoral, to be precise, and it hardly would lead the entire male population to buy grapefruits for their spouses' faces. The scene was important mostly because, though shocking, it was good for a tremendous laugh. And that scene was cut in three states. The very censors who cut it allowed a murder to be shown, they allowed the last, gruesome scene in *Public Enemy*—as grisly a thing as you'll find in pictures—to be shown, yet they wouldn't let the grapefruit go. It was funny. It was coarse and hard-boiled, but it was funny.

For the reason the New England fathers called the fiddle the devil's instrument, for the reason Prohibition officers now harass poor coal miners for making wine to drink at home—for these reasons censors are not to be regarded as gentlemanly opponents. They can make fine speeches about the children and about states' rights, but, when you get right down to it, they actually have that inner hatred of gaiety that made Anthony Comstock arrest a tailor for having the dummy of a woman in his window—they have that fire and brimstone gnawing at their vitals which makes them writhe every time they see two young people swinging down the street arm in arm. And there is no cure for these gentlemen, and there is no decent, humane way to treat them. It's a great mistake to imagine you can treat them on a legal basis. I heard Mr. John S. Sumner debate last year and he called Assemblyman Langdon Post old-fashioned, bitter names while Mr. Post did nothing but introduce a bill into the legislature politely asking that body to do away with Mr. Sumner's organization.

Rather than debate with the censors, I think we might include Prohibition fanatics and go about with a Flit sprayer full of pleasant-smelling lethal gas. It wouldn't be any more damaging to civilization than raiding struggling booksellers or cutting pictures in the privacy of offices so that a hard-working, tired citizenry may not have a chance to laugh long and heartily.

Judge, August 8, 1931

AN AMERICAN TRAGEDY

M R. DREISER, who has become pontifical in his autumnal days, tried to restrain Paramount from producing *An American Tragedy* with his title and his name attached to it, and I rather wish the producers had let him have his way and released the picture as "Love in a Factory" by Joe Zilch, or some such combination, because the picture itself is liable to be obscured by the smoke from Mr. Dreiser's damp fire, and it is worth more than that.

It is an important picture, this *An American Tragedy*, which Josef von Sternberg turned out, and not because of the novel but in spite of it. It is the first time, I believe, that the subjects of sex, birth control, and murder, all three, have been put in a picture with sense, taste, and reality. Again, it is a picture with a sociological background. Hitherto every time we have unexpected mothers on the screen, they needs must have been love slaves to Captains in His Majesty's army of this or that country, or else characters from nowhere in particular. Again, when dealing with the facts of life, movies seldom shade character. The father is the villain; the fellow who finds out about it, but eventually forgives, is the hero, and that's all there is to them.

Murder, of course, is as common as apple pie in the movies these days, and audiences have become so accustomed to this ancient pastime that they guffaw every time somebody says something about "going for a ride" and, instead of falling on his rear, the modern comedian takes a machine gun and kills twenty extras in order to get his big laugh.

Psychological murders, however, *crimes passionels*, and other realistic crimes are seldom mentioned or at least done with any sense in pictures. And while Sternberg and his author had plenty of chances to go astray with Mr. Dreiser's 700,000 words, they cleaved through the verbiage and did a simple, moving picture about a domestic murder in a small, bigoted, typical up-state manufacturing town. You may know the story.

The son of a tattered pair of mission workers eventually lands in the factory of his wealthy uncle, although he is given the social status of a poor relative. There, he encounters a country girl who works in the factory, and for several months they enjoy a childlike, simple love affair. Comes autumn, and they retire to the girl's room.

In the meantime, the boy has met the society belle of the town and for weeks he deserts his factory girl while he joins in the mad whirl of Lycurgus events. When he learns that his girl is about to be a mother, he sends her away with a promise of marriage. He eventually joins her in the country, takes her to a resort, drowns her, is discovered and, after a fine set of speeches by politically ambitious lawyers, is sentenced to death.

Sternberg is at his best with the courtroom crowds. With superb timing, he takes his camera from the stony faces of the dazed farm couple whose child went to the bottom of the lake outside to the hot-dog vendors, the sex-story publishers, and the insane townspeople, drooling with blood-lust from the stimulation of an illicit love affair and a murder. Some of the courtroom scenes become tiresome, but I imagine this is because the producers let Dreiser talk them into trying to follow his elephantine path through the jungles of small-town politics. I imagine also that the several speeches about "society" and its treatment of the hero, which seem dragged in by the ears, were inserted to please the *prima donna* of Hollywood bellyachers.

But even though the producers tried to please their author with illogical speeches, and even though they probably stuck the last scene and speech in the piece to placate the members of the D.A.R. and the various other groups who indubitably will rally to the cause of purity as soon as they have seen the show ten times, I think *An American Tragedy* is a splendid production. Phillips Holmes is a solemn, wooden young man, but he is fortunate in the earlier parts of the movie because he has Sylvia Sydney with him. I am almost embarrassed to find myself mumbling over fan-column adjectives about this young lady because you probably will begin to suspect me when you hear those old familiar chants, but I have never seen a better performance on the screen than she gives in this movie, and I never have seen a young actress who by sheer force could so dramatize scenes which otherwise might have been colorless.

For Miss Sydney alone *An American Tragedy* is worth an orchestra seat. (Miss Dee is a very, very comely gal and does her work well, but there's no use talking about the rest of the cast when you consider the work of Miss Sydney.)

I am almost sorry *An American Tragedy* is a sober, responsible picture; otherwise I should enjoy Mr. Dreiser's sullen outburst, but the picture is worthy and the elderly gentleman has climbed into bed with the many uninformed, condescending movie critics, to say nothing of cheap producers, gratuitous and paid censors, and other forms of movie hecklers.

Judge, August 15, 1931

THE CRITICS

I AM constantly amazed at the lack of intelligent, informed writing about motion pictures in this country. We have the best cameramen, we have the best directors, some of the best playwrights, and stables full of talented actors. The ownership of motion picture companies is so involved with power control that the biggest bank in the country has had to go into the picture business —to its sorrow—and the rise and fall of movies may well indicate the rise and fall of national banking and politics.

With this as material, what is written about the movies—and by whom? There are a few men working on New York daily papers who have good critical judgment, but they are so near Broadway, they have so molded and restrained their opinions of movies to a comparison of the Broadway stage, that the manifold importance of pictures is reduced by them to casual comment on daily openings. As an eighth grade child could give you a good criticism of the ordinary motion picture, the importance and value of newspaper criticism in New York come down to the writing ability of the critics. Three of them write fairly well and with a certain amount of humor.

The financial involutions of the movie industry, the censorship —and they could by law demand a list of cuts from the censors and publish them day by day—the political pressure brought to bear on the industry—none of these things is dealt with by these gentlemen.

Outside of New York, I have been unable to find a newspaper movie critic unharnessed by his advertising department, although I may have missed some good men. This year movie companies started to run commercial advertising in their theatres, and free newspapers that up to this time had let theatre owners write their movie criticisms suddenly became bold and liberal and raised the very devil because it looked as if the boys were going to take some business from them. Advertising has been discontinued by most of the companies. As far as I know these liberal newspapers have resumed their policy of letting press agents and exhibitors tell the public about Hollywood's fables.

Then there are the fan columns, all of which are alike. I haven't anything against a fan column. I myself work on a newspaper. I don't run a fan column and I get letters from moviegoers who evidently wouldn't believe one if I did. There are, of course, hundreds of people who do, but what I am getting at is this. Considering the boast of liberal newspapers, considering the number of people who write about movies, it is unbelievable that so little of it goes beyond a street-corner discussion of the latest movie star.

Recently dramatic critics have condescended to write about the lowly pictures, yet, with the exception of George Jean Nathan, who sees the pictures he talks about, and who meets them on their own ground, by their writings not one of these gentlemen has seen a picture since *Birth of a Nation.*

I believe the ordinary intelligent citizen has learned something about movie technique. I think he spots bad photography and knows when he is being bothered by cheap sound apparatus. I know that thousands of women wait for the next Constance Bennett picture (which is in itself enough reason to repeal the Nineteenth Amendment), but for these people there are the fan columns, any one of which can be written by taking a lollipop in one hand, a drink of bathtub gin in the other, and having a picture of "September Morn" pasted in front of your typewriter.

I think there are two good reasons why men who should know better fail to give the public any real information about movies. In the first place, Hollywood has been ridiculed by temperamental press agents, cast-off stage directors, and $40-a-week reporters to such an extent that most movie critics have an inferiority complex. Obviously the Shuberts, *et al.,* are a much more polished, gentlemanly class of men than those vulgar multi-millionaires on the Coast, and it is legendary that stage directors and stage producers never present a show that has not been nurtured with calm reasoning, honesty, and a maximum of talent.

In the second place, critics in these United States are notoriously illiterate and lazy. I doubt that there is a movie critic in New York —the only city where there is such a thing—who knows the fundamentals of modern photography, and I'm quite sure there is not a one who could tell you how pictures are distributed. The Germans, who can print amazing photographs in nickel magazines, publish a book a week on photography, one of which has been an enormous best-seller. The British employ movie critics who at least are familiar with some of the King's English, who travel to Switzerland and France to see pictures, who have studied photography. But our boys are too busy trying to be novelists, playwrights, or dramatic critics to bother with such things.

This is true not only of movie critics. It is true of music, literary, and dramatic critics, so don't blame the haggard gentlemen of the press. You'll only further their inferiority complexes.

Judge, August 29, 1931

WHO PUTS THE NAVY IN EVERY NEWSREEL?

T HE UNITED States Navy has become this year another confusion to me. It happens I do not consider it a major worry, otherwise it alone would be enough to cause me to fall back on my heels and gaze until oblivion at the center of my rapidly expanding stomach. Nevertheless, hardly a week goes by that some new and equivocal item regarding our brave sailor boys does not confound me.

Until reaching the age of senility and newspaper-reading I had a pretty comforting idea about the Navy. I remembered that old somebody or other said "Don't give up the ship," I remembered that we blew up the Maine and that we whipped the British, and as far as I was concerned that was enough for any Navy to do.

It was after the war that the first doubt struck me, because I happened to see what seemed to be the entire Navy relaxing in York River while the Germans were making nuisances of themselves by blowing up transports and various other valuable pieces of marine property. I was told the British Navy was doing the dirty work—perfectly fitting, seeing as how it was England's war, but I never learned, and haven't yet, what our own brave boys were doing at Hampton Roads. I know what some of them were doing, but after all, a whole Navy couldn't have been doing that at the same time.

Later, before I joined the lower orders of the writing class, a growing aesthetic attitude and a Captain McGregor made me realize that, after all, the Navy was worth all its expense because it is pretty, it is colorful, and its men do keep their ships nice and shiny when they pull into Newport, New York, and San Diego. (As they haven't done anything else but pull into Newport, San Diego, and New York for ten years to my knowledge, that gives them a pretty high rating in cleanliness and deportment.)

My necessary movie attendance has chilled my enthusiasm for the Navy on the simple grounds that it is unimaginative. For seven years, I have seen bow and stern, port and starboard of every cruiser, battleship, and sub-chaser in the service going through what the newsreels claim are maneuvers. I have seen ten thousand five hundred and ninety pursuit planes lay smoke screens for these same ships—another maneuver which puzzles me, because a small boy with a pea gun should be able to shut his eyes, aim at the smoke screen and hit one of the ships. I also have seen a few grim shots of sunken submarines, extravagantly lost with men and expensive machinery because some restless admiral wanted the boys to do something besides walk up and down Riverside Drive.

Until last year, I still had no definite resentment against the Navy; I simply was bored with the newsreel shots. Since then, however, all sorts of things have happened. Hoover, I was told, had cut the Navy in two. He had reduced its pay, scrapped its battleships. Endless copy was written about a naval conference, the very headlines giving me a terrific headache. All of a sudden a very fierce gentleman was investigated; Charlie Schwab had to hustle to Washington and explain what interest the Bethlehem Steel Company had in the Navy, and the once polite and pretty service began to be, in my eyes, something conceived by Oppenheim and Conrad, with spies, provocateurs, and intrigues.

As though that were not enough, somebody said Mr. Hoover didn't even know the names of the battleships, or something, and the President had to appoint a committee to call somebody a liar.

I thought, and hoped, that that would be the end of the Navy in the news. But no. They are re-making some cruisers which unfortunately don't steer or float very well. Furthermore, the Navy has a new airship. And last but not least, it helped make a fairly exciting cheap melodrama called *Hell Divers* in which Wallace Beery and Clark Gable impersonate two loud-talking service fliers. Everything but Washington's monument was used in the picture. And the flying, although overdone, is exciting.

The picture is, to my mind, exciting propaganda for the Navy. The point is: Who puts the Navy in every newsreel? Why? Who wants a big Navy? Are they scrapping battleships or building them? Are they building up the flying corps or are they using the money to build submarines that won't submerge? Have we got as good a submarine as the new German one? Why can't we build ships as powerful as Germany's pocket cruiser? Who cares about the Navy anyway, and if so, what good, other than its undeniably pleasant customs and color, is the darn Navy? To anyone who can answer these questions truthfully, clearly, and politely, I shall be glad to give two tickets to *Hell Divers* and my deep thanks. I'm tired of being confused about everything.

Judge, January 23, 1932

TAXI

I SEE by the papers that Major General Harbord and Martin Littleton, Jr., head a committee which is going to aid the courts of Kentucky and other cultural bodies in a desperate fight to drive Communism or any other form of political thought of even a pale pink tone from the country. General Harbord is closely connected with the Radio Corporation, which is in the picture business, so I think it is not unwise if I call the attention of his committee to the insidious, antisocial, and undermining political propaganda now rife in motion pictures.

This propaganda goes forth to the world it molds, as Mr. Hays put it so nicely, that "virgin thing, that unmarked slate, the mind of a child." And see what impressions have been marked on that slate recently! *Taxi* is a good example. A Mr. James Cagney is now a popular movie hero. In this picture he is a cabdriver. But he does not work for General Motors or the Parmelee System, and this is where you should take note, General. He is the leader of an independent group of taxi drivers who fight a corporation! As the hero of this un-American business group, he goes about punching people in the jaw and he is unmannerly and un-American in his attitude to his fiancée, even trying right hooks to her fair chin. But, worst of all, he sets out to avenge a pal who was murdered by, not a Russian, or an N.Y.U. assistant professor, but by a gangster, corporation-employed!

In fact, he takes the law into his own hands, as Soviet and as distasteful an idea as you can imagine, General, and almost commits a murder for vengeance. Even after he is stopped by policemen, he is allowed to go his way unharmed!

Of course, a few of us understand that *Taxi* is fiction of the wildest variety, and that it is meant merely to be amusing. It really was amusing to me, General, and I never once believed that the authors or actors of the picture meant us to believe that corporations hire killers to put down competition or that independent business groups actually are allowed to prosper and operate in these days— we know better than that, General—but I do think such plots, even when amusing, may put little seeds of doubt into the virgin minds of our children, and I have no doubt that your committee will be able to get Mr. Hays to see eye to eye with you.

For the parents who may want to see *Taxi* after the kiddies have come home from the poolroom and gone to bed, my judgment is that you will find it an amusing, rough-and-tumble comedy as pleasing as the previous productions we have had from authors Glasman and Bright, and actor Cagney.

Judge, February 6, 1932

ARROWSMITH

Because it was dramatized by a reputable man, because it was given care and time, and because it had movie possibilities, I naturally believed the boys when they raved about *Arrowsmith*, when they pronounced it the finest thing the movies have shown us. You can imagine my surprise when I discovered that it was very mediocre entertainment, when I found direction of not even a fair order, and when I discovered that Mr. Colman, who was miscast, ignored or was unable to see a great opportunity, and portrayed Martin Arrowsmith as a toff in what Mr. Lonsdale calls drawing-room comedy.

I have read the Lewis novel several times. I always have believed it his best book, and I regard Leora Arrowsmith as the one Lewis heroine who was given glamour and charm by her maker. The novel covered so much ground that I felt, when I heard Mr. Howard was to adapt it for the movies, that his job would prove difficult.

"The one thing you have to do with a novel is to forget it and start afresh." I offer Mr. Howard the observation of the late but excellent critic, Mr. Walkley, and I can come even closer to home and quote two sage ancients, Mr. Poe and Mr. Nathan, who have warned against adaptations. Mr. Howard did not forget the novel. Neither, unfortunately, did he remember it very well.

He starts us with Arrowsmith and Gottlieb. We meet the old scientist, and we gather, fleetingly, that he is important, that he has impressed the young Arrowsmith. We next see the hero interning in a hospital. We see him woo, and quickly marry. We see him set up in practice in South Dakota. And for a few minutes Mr. Howard gives us a good picture of the joy, the excitement, and the fears of a young doctor. He also shows us a brave heroine.

At this point, Ronald Colman lets Mr. Howard and Mr. Lewis go their ways while he goes the way of all movie actors, because, while Mr. Howard intended him to be a scientist, with small-town life smothering him, Mr. Colman, in pleated pants, goes about doctoring cows as though they were installed in a city club, and when he does get his bid to come to Gottlieb, the audience could just as well imagine him to be a traveling salesman, a member of the Anti-Red Patriots of Idaho, or the second violinist in a crooning orchestra, as a scientist.

The Institute scenes are practically meaningless. I do not know whether the McDuff Institute, its people, its politics, and its work bored Mr. Howard, or whether, knowing it was intended by Mr. Lewis and Mr. De Kruif to be a keen picture of the Rockefeller Institute, the movie executives were afraid to bear down on it and give the audience a disillusioning picture of scientists at home, and therefore restrained Mr. Howard. Whatever the reason, the main part of the picture, Arrowsmith's struggles in New York, his belated discovery of a serum, his devotion to Gottlieb, his affection for his partner—these things are indicated but not dramatized; they are so barely indicated that one not familiar with the novel must wonder at them.

Of course, these scenes take time. Mr. Howard couldn't put the novel intact on the screen.

Arrowsmith is a long picture. I have taken you almost to the intermission, and up to this point the director has done nothing. He simply set up his camera and photographed what Mr. Howard wrote. After the intermission, the director evidently became inspired, because he rushed a bunch of Negro extras onto a set which looks as though it had been left for the latest version of *White Cargo*, and began to make a motion picture. But just when Miss Helen Hayes was furnishing him with some of the best acting he or any other director will ever have, just when you begin to feel the heat, the death in the tropics, just when Arrowsmith begins to grow in stature and importance, Director Ford and Mr. Howard suddenly insert a menace in the form of a well-dressed woman, and she and Mr. Colman moon at each other while Miss Hayes dies in vain. The drama, the tension of the scene evaporates, and the audience begins to wonder about Mr. Colman and the menace. That there was such a character in the novel had nothing to do with the picture. It was rank carelessness on the part of Mr. Howard to fiddle with this minor character just when he was killing his heroine; it was stupidity on the part of the director, because any director worth his salt should have seen the potentialities of Leora's death.

Helen Hayes, Richard Bennett, and A. E. Anson give *Arrowsmith* some importance. They are magnificent. The novel plot, the fact that the picture was intended to be important, gives it, in this day of bedroom melodramas, further weight. But Mr. Howard and Mr. Ford showed no movie sense, shot poor Arrowsmith in the back, and I conclude with genuine bewilderment: What was all the shouting for, boys?

Judge, February 13, 1932

MOVIE MUSIC

WITH rare exceptions, Hollywood directors have not tried to use music with motion pictures. Even Lubitsch has given up, and when he makes a musical picture he is content to let the music take the place of pictures. In *One Hour With You*, he does develop a pleasant intimacy by having Chevalier speak asides to the audience, but this is just a pleasant trick; he never lets the movie appear to spring from the music.

Once he did—one scene in *Monte Carlo*—when he had the peasants singing and swaying in the fields to the tempo of the music, which in turn was geared to the motion of the train. As a scene, it was perfect, but he never has built a movie on this idea, an idea which, in my opinion, offers the only genuine future movies will have, if anything has a future these days.

It is true that, with the exception of the British, we are the least musical people in the world, but that should not influence a director. Properly handled, music should be knit into a film so that the audience is no more aware of it than it is of the dimmed house lights or the actors' greasepaint. The directors who do not fear public ignorance are themselves handicapped by not knowing or caring for music.

A movie director, in fact, should be an artist, a crack photogra-

pher, a musician, a playwright, and a director. And this is no ambiguous equation, applicable to all artisans. For instance, Von
Sternberg is a crack photographer and he has used music exceed-
ingly well. On the other hand, he can't tell a play from a two-line
joke and while his productions always are interesting, they seldom
have any form or clarity.

Lubitsch knows music and he is a good director and an excellent
photographer. He doesn't go any further with his musical productions simply because, I imagine, he has hit on a successful formula
and he is going to keep to it.

Judge, June 11, 1932

A NOUS LA LIBERTE

RENE Clair's *A Nous la Liberté* is a French musical picture with
so little dialogue you need not worry for fear Junior, who had
to take a business course because he couldn't pass freshman English, will not understand the proceedings. (I say this in spite of
the fact that the distinguished critic of our more reserved metropolitan daily called the manager of the Europa Theatre seven
times before he wrote his review, asking to have various points of
the complicated comedy explained.)

A Nous la Liberté represents the first graduate work of the only
movie director in France who is worth the price of a German
bond. It is typically French, insofar as the writings of Maugham
could be called typically British or Jerome Kern's music could be
called typically American. There is a delicacy, a flavor, and a certain childishness about the picture which one would not find in
the work of any other nationality. However, for all this France
has not given many directors to the world and it is Monsieur Clair
himself who has fought with the camera until he makes it do more
for him than for ninety percent of the German, Russian, and
Anglo-Saxon directors of long experience.

You will, perhaps, find it merely a deft light comedy with strong evidences of the old Keystone cop pictures in it. If you look with any sort of discerning eye you will find more—you will find one fundamental principle of moviemaking employed in every scene. That is, every agency of the talking picture is employed every minute. Clair has learned from his elders. Do the Russians take beautiful nature studies? Very well. Clair sets his camera down in a wheat field and gives you a lovely glimpse of heavy-headed stalks swaying lightly in the wind. Laurel and Hardy have modernized the custard pie slapstick. Good enough. Clair's comedians kick each other in the pants and instigate chases up and down boulevards. But these sequences are not tossed desperately into the mill; they are deftly placed to give variety, pace, and spice, and they are so expertly knit into the picture that you feel, after you have seen it, almost as though you had watched an artisan engrave a vase, or seen a cabinetmaker swiftly knock together a fragile piece of furniture.

This very fragility, in fact, is my one objection to A Nous La Liberté. There are times when the discreet satire seems almost too gentle, when the factory, which is so clean and charming and modern, seems more like an exhibit of modern art than an inorganic monster eating away at its human food, but this probably is a reflection of my own diet rather than a criticism of the picture. I am not French, and one's nerves become rather numb after a decade of civic alarums, city traffic, lightning cocktails, and the other loud manifestations of our local kulture. If you don't enjoy the delicate satire, it is for the same reason that you probably can't drink good wine or read anything but picture papers.

The story is one that has been staring our own moviemakers in the face for ten years. As I have frequently remarked before, those gentlemen who step on The Chief and ride across a continent every month know only three locales: Los Angeles, Chicago, New York—three cities which have as little to do with these United States as a carnival barker has to do with the towns upon which his show descends.

Searching desperately for material, they transport rheumatic British hacks, they employ emigrés to tell them about court life in old Vienna, while all the time the most fantastic, violent, barbaric, careless, and altogether monstrous community in North America —I refer to Detroit—squats on Lake Michigan, waiting.

Clair, living in a country which never, so long as a Frenchman has a franc under the mattress, will succumb to the machine age, nevertheless has delivered a pictorial horselaugh to Moscow and Detroit and their factory philosophy. Do we have to wait for the Germans and even the Italians to take advantage of the exciting pictures waiting in great factories in Pittsburgh, Detroit, and Gary?

Clair starts with a prison workshop. To the tinkle of pleasant music, we see two comrades planning a prison break. One of them succeeds in getting away, and in quick flashes we see him rise from a street hawker to the management of a huge phonograph factory. The other comrade eventually is released from prison. Wandering in childish nonchalance on the trail of a girl he has seen, he finds himself working in the factory assembly room which is disciplined just like the prison. Eventually the childish one, who finds working no more fun than prison life, meets his old friend, now surrounded with all the trappings of big business. From this point on, you anticipate the denouement, but you do not care. The music is gay, the pictures are lovely, and every so often Clair turns his boys loose for an old cop chase, with much kicking in the pants. (Some of these scenes might have been cut, but the actors seem to enjoy their sprints and I don't think you will cavil with them.) At the end we find the factory occupied by pinochle players and the two comrades, broke and contented, taking to the road.

I hope the Messrs. Stalin and Eisenstein, along with the American-Russian Institute, the editors of The Nation, and Mr. Ford are fortunate enough to see A Nous la Liberté. At least I hope you do. You will find a rare combination—a director unmolested by sales managers or supervisors, who has successfully combined music and pictures to work out a natural movie story, with two charming actors to help him. You can't ask for any more in the way of a motion picture.

Judge, June 18, 1932

STRANGE INTERLUDE

THE FILM version of *Strange Interlude* will cause professional and amateur critics alike to flood the public prints with a routine fallacious stream of comment, furiously debating such unimportant considerations as: Is the movie as good as the play? Is Gable an actor? Has Norma Shearer become a great emotional actress? Does the picture mark a new era of Art in Hollywood? And so on.

That it was a courageous thing to dismantle the giant structure of the play and put it together in a picture, that seldom do we have such material assembled on the screen, is of importance only to those who like to point with pride to landmarks of progress as we whiz by them.

However, it did take courage to screen a play which cuts with deep surgical strokes into its characters; a play, certainly, whose characters struggle so much more earnestly and terribly than any ever put on a screen that there is no other movie with which to compare it. But, while courage is rare enough in movie circles, the producers needed more than that. They were faced with the almost insoluble problem of adapting one medium to another. They were faced with a play which on the stage ran for five hours, a playing time impossible for the screen. (Impossible, that is, if they wanted to make expenses.) And they had a play which demands the best, and more, from the best actors.

Once committed to the job, the producers cannily refused to trifle with these details. They simply threw O'Neill into the hands of a crew of Hollywood workers who heretofore had aimed their efforts directly at the hearts of those people who are privy to Brisbane, Louella Parsons, and the domestic life of Clara Bow, and hoped they would wrest from the manuscript a picture which would startle the stenographers, appease the hecklers, and delight the ladies' culture clubs. They employed C. Gardner Sullivan and Bess Meredyth to rewrite O'Neill, they allowed Robert Leonard to direct the picture, and they gathered together an extraordinary group of actors to play in it—Henry B. Walthall, May Robson,

Ralph Morgan, Clark Gable, Norma Shearer, Alexander Kirkland, Robert Young, and Maureen O'Sullivan.

You might reasonably expect the worst from such a crew. Actually, they produced another Hollywood paradox: a movie which is far better than it has any right to be.

The scenario writers may have been overawed or dismayed into incomprehension by the manuscript; they did little to it except jam the whole play, curtains, dinner hour and all, into two hours' playing time. They cut only a few of the lines which in every movie since *Bronco Billy* have been considered taboo. They did, of course, destroy the delicate balance, the extraordinary symmetry of the play, but it had to be cut, and no one could have done much better. They completely destroyed the character of Charlie and censored his repeated explanations of his sexual fixation. They also cut most of his poetic asides, yet it was a fortunate procedure, because had they chiseled from each character, there would have been little left.

The many asides offered difficulties, but they were handled in a way which makes the picture. As you will remember, on the stage the characters "froze" when an aside was spoken; in the movie the characters play in pantomime while the asides are spoken into a microphone off-screen. At times, they are monotonous or theatrical, but once the picture is under way they seem natural and until the last two acts this mechanical construction gradually eliminates the actors. When the asides, which contain the poetry and the drama of the play, are spoken, you gradually lose sight of the cast. You feel only the grim, terse metre of the words, you feel their complete impact unfiltered or halted by actors' gesture or articulation, you feel they are obeying unseen Delphic commands; and had the play been designed for the screen and not for the stage, we would have had a simple, easy combination of silent and sound picture potentiality.

The play was not designed for the screen and as a result you feel rushed; although it plays for two hours, the characters live an emotional lifetime. Whereas the play had the steady beat of a heroic funeral march, linking Nina and Ned and Sam and Uncle Charlie to a lockstep in which they march inevitably to their graves, the picture is content to push them into a quick dogtrot.

However, O'Neill is always there. He surmounts Kirkland, a likely juvenile miscast as the hail-fellow-well-met businessman. He surmounts endless close-ups, which give you the feeling at times that you are watching a picture through the wrong end of a telescope. (He can, unfortunately, hardly surmount Ralph Morgan as Charlie, because his character was changed into a comic female impersonator, a distortion which Mr. Morgan does little to correct.)

Cut, miserably cast, and photographed with a minimum of imagination, it is difficult to believe that a great play could be at all important in such a translation. Yet the off-screen asides occasionally give *Strange Interlude* a flow it did not have on the stage, and at no time, despite scenes which are unpointed and meaningless—particularly that great one in which Nina sits at the table saying, "These are my men," a scene which in dim light on the stage seemed a weird savage mystical ceremony, and which in the movie is chastened into a conventional speech—at no time do you feel that you are watching a reproduced stage play.

It is also amazing that such incompetent actors did so little damage. It is only in the last two acts that you become aware of them. In these lamentable minutes you do suddenly realize that Miss Shearer is up to her old tricks, tricks which have been known to send docile husbands home to beat their children and snap at their wives; you do see in a flash that Clark Gable, burdened under ten pounds of powder, looks like a minor character in a George Washington pageant, and that Alexander Kirkland, with a pillow stuck in his middle, looks like a small boy playing Napoleon at Elba.

Yet this very childish incompetence is perhaps a fortunate thing for us. Had the producers sent man-sized people to struggle with the script, we might have been the losers. They might have wrenched *Strange Interlude* away from O'Neill. As it is, they put up no battle, and he and the audience win easily.

The picture will probably be a tremendous success. It marks no epoch, it forwards no specific movie form, it proves, in fact, nothing except that *Strange Interlude* is one of the finest plays of our time. But it is more exciting than a thousand "action" movies and it does, in my opinion, give you a truer interpretation of the play than the country at large was given by a weary road company of stage actors.

Vanity Fair, September, 1932

BALLYHOO

IT HAS been an almost world-wide contention that only backward children and paroled convicts go to the movies, and it is more than possible that the carpers and the executives, who seem to work hand in hand, have been right.

While right now, as usual, there are enough pictures on the market to convince any Conservative member of Parliament that American movies are responsible for the decline of the pound, the Chinese trouble, and Herbert Hoover, there are also a few pictures which, while not to be stacked alongside the major dramatic conceptions of the last century, are at least pleasant and sufficiently mature in their point of view to appeal to quite a few grown people. But, and this is the point, I wonder if the producers and the advertising managers and the managing editors of newspapers ever once thought to understand just how these adults are to distinguish between a piece of sour hokum such as *Blonde Captive* and, say, *Love Me Tonight*.

For instance, I have before me a morning paper with a page full of advertisements. I find these restrained notices to the public: "The Greatest Picture That Chevalier's Ever Played In! . . . From all over the country they came, they saw, they were conquered by the most brilliant entertainment in 25 years!"

Now it just happens that *Love Me Tonight* is an excellent picture, a picture distinguished by a demonstration of surprising skill by Rouben Mamoulian, and made more pleasant by a good musical score furnished by Richard Rodgers. But how in the name of Heaven could any citizen of this city expect such a refreshing surprise when he is asked to follow the judgment of Miss Hazel Flynn of Chicago, Mr. Jack Moffett of Kansas City, or Mr. Meier of Cleveland?

I hasten to say that I do not know the works of any one of these stellar newspaper reviewers. My point is, why should anyone in New York be interested in reading that these imported reviewers had found that "feminine eyes will shine . . . male pulses will pump," that the film was "terrific" . . . "one of the truly great pictures of all time" when one of their own bright performers, Miss Carewe, had only a few months ago written that *Shanghai Express* was "the greatest picture in ten years."

It is true that *Love Me Tonight* is well worth the price of admission. But if the producer can do nothing but quote a daily reviewer's "terrific," a procedure which he has followed week in and week out for years, how, I repeat, does he expect to inform a large part of the public that his picture is really pretty good and not just another sell, as have been most of the "terrifics" in times past?

This calliope manner of ballyhoo is carried on in the theatre and, should anyone like to examine them, I have a few letters from regular movie customers complaining about the length, stupidity, and blatancy of the so-called trailer used for advance advertising. I recall that for *High Pressure* the producers were content to advertise on the screen that William Powell would "steal money from the men and kisses from the ladies," an announcement which probably kept lots of people home. Actually, *High Pressure* was a good farce full of amusing incidents. It was only by luck that the movie customer ever found it out. Certainly he couldn't judge from the advertising.

A double example of stupid salesmanship occurred in the titling of *Million Dollar Legs*. I avoided it for weeks until finally I decided to go just to see W. C. Fields. Much to my surprise, I found it a fairly amusing picture, and one that might have been a genuine fantasy had not the author been allowed to let a good comedy idea fall into mechanical, labored situations. As it is, the picture has Fields as the president of a nation of athletes, it has the adept Lyda Roberti in an excellent take-off of Garbo, and yet I can't imagine the casual customer would think the picture was anything more than a story about the leading lady of a foreign bagnio who is rescued by a fresh-faced American college boy who learns that true love surpasses pot luck.

Fortunately, comedies stump the movie sales magi. There isn't much they can say about the Four Marx Brothers that the brothers don't say for themselves. *Horsefeathers* is a great deal like their other plays and is built on the same framework. However, I, for one, enjoyed it and Perelman and Ruby and Kalmar have given Groucho some new gags, and the brothers have found a sturdy blonde to wrestle with for a great part of the time in their usual unrestrained manner. Most people by now are acquainted with the Marx Brothers' shows, and those who like them will not need much advertising to induce them to the theatre. Fortunately, however, the producer didn't call the thing *Their Sin* and advertise it as a tragedy of college life, which would not have been much more fantastic than titling a comedy about the Olympic games *Million Dollar Legs*. Legs in this country have only one gender.

Judge, September 15, 1932

LOVE ME TONIGHT

HAVING sold the public down the river a hundred times over by shouting "hosannah!" for every piece of junk with a star in the cast that comes out of the movie studios, the daily reviewers finally have a picture which gives them some reason to cheer; and should the cries of "powerful," "magnificent," "stupendous" quoted in the papers have kept you away from this picture, you can turn back and find *Love Me Tonight* worth your money. It is a gay, attractive, melodious movie.

In spirit and form, it owes much to René Clair and F. W. Murnau, the only movie directors who ever properly blended music and pictures. However, unlike his contemporaries, Rouben Mamoulian, who made *Love Me Tonight*, was not content to imitate the Europeans. He simply applied the fundamental principle used by them and, with the aid of a pleasant story, a good musician, a talented cast and about a million dollars, he has done what someone in Hollywood should have done long ago—he has illustrated a musical score.

From the opening scene, there are at least a dozen times when you are almost convinced that here is just another musical production brightened with some clever lines and some pleasant acting. You are quickly disillusioned. This ancient scene—Paris at dawn, time after time a prelude to a grinding story of how love came to a dissolute artist and a little girl from Pine Bluffs—turns into an exciting, carefully prepared crescendo.

You see, as of yore, the chimneys swept with morning mist. A bell tolls the hour. A workman appears, throws his pick to the ground, and starts to work. A chambermaid appears, glances at the sky, and sweeps her doorstep. You hear the bang of the pick, the swish of the broom. A cobbler sets up his last and pegs at his shoes. Bang, swish, crack—and then the music fades in and gradually the city wakes up in the orchestra until, finally, with chimneys smoking, hucksters crying their goods, cabs cawing at one another, the orchestra in a loud crash provides a raucous, lively entrance for Monsieur Chevalier, who gets out of bed, opens the window, and sings a little chorus to the city.

The opening scene is carried on too long, and the singers force their gaiety, but it is thoroughly done and it is an indication of the good sweep of the show. Once under way, Mamoulian never lets go, and after this opening chorus, he presents his songs in better order and balance. Long before the pleasant finale, you realize that suddenly the former stage director has hit his stride; that once rid of his marble busts, his symbolic nonsense, and his amateur preoccupation with camera angles, he has conceived and produced a fortunate, charming musical picture.

The music itself half explains the excellence of the production. It is an unusual score, not merely a collection of songs with incidental orchestrations dubbed into the picture haphazardly. Every measure of the score is scrupulously arranged to fit the picture and, more important, Richard Rodgers has written some sound music and some melodies that surpass even the music he wrote for the unfortunate "Chee-Chee." His partner Hart, not to be outdone, has written some lyrics which would be a gift to any musical comedy. With such a score to start with, Mamoulian made good use of every note.

There is plenty for him to use, and I wish they had recapitulated some of the incidental music, but Rodgers was generous and even the title song is used only a few times and never hauled from the picture and jammed into the camera by Chevalier or Mac-Donald or a chorus. It is in his appreciation of the score and his adroit use of it that Mamoulian proves how quickly he has learned since his first three experiments at picture making. He seldom allows Miss MacDonald to do anything but sing. She can do that, and thus we are spared the painful experience of seeing her demonstrate her rather bovine sense of comedy. Chevalier is prevented from being too, too ingratiating and is thereby a much more pleasing and valuable player.

There is a lusty spirit manifest in the whole show and even the minor players who, after all, include Joseph Cawthorne, C. Aubrey Smith, and Elizabeth Patterson, manage to give you a feeling of exuberance. Charles Butterworth is given some material and room enough for a real comic characterization; Myrna Loy is for once melted down to an easy natural manner, which makes her twice as comely; but, from start to finish, *Love Me Tonight*, which by now you might judge is an entertaining picture, is the result of Mamoulian's perspicacity.

We will, of course, now suffer a barrage of musical pictures. And, when you consider it, there is no trick to the thing. A good score, some actors, a simple tale, and a director who understands how to put them all together—almost any corporation should be able to produce as much. There is, of course, one requirement. Someone must know in advance whether the music and the tale and the director are any good.

Vanity Fair, October, 1932

I AM A FUGITIVE

THERE were two ways in which Director LeRoy could have made *I Am a Fugitive*. He could have ripped the highlights from the startling novel of the same name, written by a convict escaped from the chain gang, and told in brief episodes the story of this man's life. As the story is a horrible one, he could have used the man as an instrument against his background and, like the Germans and Russians at their best, manipulated people as group actors, making the prison, and not the actors, the object of the film.

Unfortunately, he had to expect a profit from his labors and try at once to tell a dramatic story and still to dramatize his hero, and he certainly did not soften the background. But in doing this he failed to characterize the brutal guards, the horrible complacency of state officials, their utter detachment from society.

I don't hold with the radical school of critics that indignation *per se* is art. However, I don't join hands with the arty boys, either, who maintain that all indignation is cheap and inartistic simply because it attempts to grind an ax. Actually, *I Am a Fugitive* is not a moralizing treatise. But you can't see it without feeling that it is a savage document against existing penal systems, nor can you ignore daily evidence that such systems are operating in our great commonwealths every day in the week.

I quarrel with the production not because it is savage and horrible, but because each step in an inevitable tragedy is taken clumsily, and because each character responsible for the hero's doom is shown more as a caricature than as a person. The men do not seem real. The chain gang certainly does. You may very well say you want to go to the theatre to forget trouble. But *I Am a Fugitive* is no moral treatise. Personally, I think you'll find it more dramatic than, say, a current play dealing with Chinese peasants, or Irish drunkards, or French maids, or middle-class neurotics.

Vanity Fair, December, 1932

MOVIE CRAZY; HORSEFEATHERS

A FTER waiting until they put Capone away before reluctantly abandoning gangster heroes, some of the producers have turned to the one real *metier* of the movie, comedy, and as a result, all at once, we are presented with Harold Lloyd, the Four Marx Brothers, and Keaton and Durante.

There is nothing funny about Harold Lloyd. He has actually not the slightest sense of comedy. He is not a mimic. His manner suggests nothing so much as that of a live-wire insurance salesman, and since talking pictures allowed him to speak, he has developed a high, squeaky, offensive manner of talking. Yet, next to Chaplin, he is the best known and most popular comedian in the world. He is a multimillionaire and a shrewd movie producer, and all because long ago he learned a few things: i.e., rustics and a large part of the world will laugh at anyone who (1) falls on his rear, (2) is kicked in the same spot, (3) is hit over the head with a hard instrument, (4) makes a fool of himself over a girl.

I never have particularly enjoyed Granma's boy because of his barber shop sentiment and his barnyard gags, but in *Movie Crazy* he again manifests his shrewd business sense, and, aware that the world moves, he has very little of Ma and Pa and quite a bit of Constance Cummings. What dialogue there is has been furnished by Vincent Lawrence, which accounts for the fact that the love scenes are charming and much more sophisticated than anything hitherto attempted by Mr. Lloyd, inasmuch as Mr. Lawrence writes about the best love scenes to be found in these parts, and this quality, added to Lloyd's usual good slapstick direction, makes it superior to anything he has done in talking pictures.

He seized for his latest production the handiest current movie plot, which is none other than that hardy story, *Merton of the Movies*. While trying to get into movies in typical Merton fashion, he has an encounter with a magician (which, after all, was funny in Chaplin's *Circus*); he has fun breaking glass every time he visits a producer's office (which was just as funny in Keaton's *The*

Cameraman); and he trips over furniture and makes love to Constance Cummings (who is an attractive young woman and whose lines were written by Mr. Lawrence). If I didn't suffer every minute for fear Mr. Lloyd would take two steps forward, smile, and try to sell me some oil stock, and if he would lower his voice into the middle register, I could again see *Movie Crazy* and consider it an hour well spent.

Which brings us to the Marx Brothers and *Horsefeathers*, their new picture. It is accurate enough to say they do nothing new in this one, but if they did anything novel they wouldn't be the Marx Brothers. You either like them or you don't. I like them, but nothing could be more painful than a description of a Marx Brothers show, so I simply advise you that Groucho has a new set of horrible puns, equally as good as the ones he last used, that S. J. Perelman furnished him a canoe scene as funny as anything they ever have had in a show, that the action takes place in a college, as well as in the inevitable boudoir, and that Harpo and Chico again make use of musical instruments.

Vanity Fair, October, 1932

VISIT TO THE MUSIC HALL

As clearly as I can remember it, this is what happened. I learned from an advertisement in the evening papers that the Radio City RKO Rockefeller Center Music Hall would open a new program at ten o'clock in the morning. I wanted to see the picture as soon as possible; consequently I arrived at the theatre at ten o'clock of a brisk, clear wintry morning. Actually, it was a little before ten, yet there were several hundred people shivering in line, herded two abreast by brocaded ushers.

I went around the corner, drank some coffee and read the morning papers, and at ten-fifteen tried again to get into the theatre. The crowd had increased perceptibly, and I asked an usher when he was going to let them in out of the cold wind. "Ten-thirty," he said. I argued incoherently with him—for some reason I can't see an usher herding people into line without wishing that I could blow a whistle and have a squadron of cavalry wheel into the mob and cut away for me—and I went around to a side entrance and discovered a sign which said, "Doors open at eleven." By this time there were several policemen detailed to keep the crowd off Sixth Avenue, and curiosity seekers were jamming the entrances, but I took an usher by the arm, pointed to the sign on the door, and asked him to explain the announcement in the daily papers.

"It must have been a misprint," he said. While I cursed myself for leaving a warm bed at such an hour in the first place, I wanted to be accurate, so I bought all the morning papers. In big type they announced that the theatre would open at ten. I immediately called Radio Pictures, and the really courteous gentleman there told me they had no control over the theatre management. I then called the theatre management and they said they had nothing to do with newspaper advertising. They did, however, offer to let me into the theatre.

I went to a mysterious entrance and found myself in a jovial crowd of rustic-looking people of all ages and sizes, all waiting to get into the theatre through the entrails of the building. We were let off somewhere in the middle of the huge auditorium, led through Roxy's private apartment by mistake, and finally let out into the Music Hall.

The stage was full of people. The vice-directors, lacking the dictatorship of Roxy himself, were rehearsing the new stage show. First the lights would go down, and a stringy-haired lean girl was spotted rising from the floor to the tune of Ravel's "Bolero." I shan't describe her idiotic interpretation of it, or dwell on the chromium sets or the Negro dance routines which so fittingly set off the music. We were watching what proved to be the grand finale, and the great denouement was furnished by sixty drummers who walked halfway into the audience and pounded out deafening metric beats to accompany the eighty-piece orchestra.

The girls were out of step, the lights didn't work, and the cymbal player was off beat, but, worst of all, no two drummers kept time.

There must have been three men, a lady dance director, and half a dozen assistants screaming at the stage performers, and there were at least four hecklers in the orchestra pit. (Of course, from where we were in the first mezzanine, we might have misunderstood—maybe they were members of a claque—but they were making a big noise about something.)

To put down only the facts, at exactly eleven forty-five, the directors gave up in despair, ordered the drummers to report to a studio somewhere to beat the drums some more, and the doors opened to over two thousand people, who, immediately they had stampeded to their seats, were entertained by an organ solo, accompanied by color pictures of some interesting cliffs. We then saw a motion picture called *Our Betters*, an interpretation of the Maugham play which was first produced in 1917 and which in its new version has been changed from an outmoded satire into a pointless comedy featuring the queen of the cuties, Constance Bennett.

Hours later, when I finally staggered out into daylight. I was puzzled to decide upon what had most impressed me about the morning: the shivering, patient, bovine people who risked pneumonia in line without a word of protest; the extravagant, irresponsible structure of picture management in general; the tragic waste of musicians, eighty of them, who labored and strained at a drab, turgid, Jew's harp interpretation of a fair piece of music; the childlike frenzy of the dance directorate, striving to get as many people to make as much noise as possible on the biggest stage in the world to accompany a tinkly, fragile piece of music; or the electrician, who, at the very end of the rehearsal, stuck his head out of his box and in a quiet, bitter tone, told the orchestra leader specifically where he could put his finale.

I do know that *Our Betters* was twisted from satire to farce, which makes it a more satisfactory, because less outmoded, play; but which also leaves the heroine without a character or a reason for being. And, even if there was some point to the character, Constance Bennett, by her invariable interpretation of a chorus girl elevated to a big part, would have destroyed it.

Judge, December 7, 1932

A FAREWELL TO ARMS

You can tell, usually, when for some mysterious reason a producer has made up his mind (or has had it made up for him by some earnest worker) to do an honest movie, when, that is, he has said, "This is a good story, shoot the works—this is a good play, etc., make it as she stands."

From all indications, this was what happened when the boys started to work on A Farewell to Arms, and that they did not make it as honest as they wanted to, is not, this time, entirely the fault of the executives.

Hemingway is the most borrowed-from fellow in contemporary literature. His terse metre has inspired a school of scenario writing. His best book, "A Farewell to Arms," is masculine and heroic; it has a charming, poignant love story in it; it has a Victorian chase and denouement which, put together, make it perfect material for movies.

I advise you at once that A Farewell to Arms is a good movie, that Helen Hayes will have the customers knee-deep in tears, and that the adapters kept as much of Hemingway's dialogue in the story as necessity allowed, showing, incidentally, good judgment in the dialogue which they did select from the novel—dialogue which, when it comes out suddenly, lifts the entire production into brisk drama.

That all the dialogue is not original Hemingway and that there are several confused and palpably false scenes may be explained simply: (1) the Italian government objected to the section of the book which showed a recent army of theirs in retreat; (2) had some sections of the novel been put on the screen the police of a hundred cities would have closed the show—and here I do not see why the producer should have risked a half million dollars for the sake of a few simple four-letter words.

Of course, you cannot twist a fine dramatic piece out of shape and expect it to retain its original power. Fortunately, Helen Hayes does all one could ask with her job. She catches the mood of her heroine perfectly, and, as Catherine Barclay is one of the loveliest heroines in modern fiction, I do not see how she could have convinced the customers any more strongly.

The simple tale, as I said, has been changed to please Mussolini, which, I suppose, is something. In the book Henry is caught up in a headlong retreat in which the officers are stopped in their tracks and shot down like dogs. But he manages to escape and decides that he is through with the Italians and that he and his sweetheart will go away together and wait for the war to end. This has been changed in the movie by a cheap device in which Rinaldi, who has to step out of his likable character, withholds letters from the hero, and this becomes the reason for the hero's desertion. Oddly enough, the whole Italian army seems to be deserting with him, so we can imagine either that the producer meant us to believe that all the other boys were going back to see what had happened to their mail, or that he originally showed the retreat and then had to cut it because of the sensitive Duce.

Even this defalcation does not really destroy all the strength of the show. Menjou makes a charming Rinaldi, and the death scene is original Hemingway—and just about his best. Director Borzage almost spoiled a good job by releasing some pigeons and bringing in the Armistice just to make his heroine's death significant, but this is just a bit of sour lemon at the very bottom of the glass. Compared with any other production you can name, A Farewell to Arms is bold, uncompromising, and adapted with the greatest respect for the author's work. And Helen Hayes gives a truly fine performance.

Judge, January 23, 1933

CAVALCADE

THERE ARE two, possibly three, reasons why every newspaper reviewer in the Eastern United States went wild with enthusiasm over *Cavalcade*, and called it everything from "the finest picture ever made in the English language" to "a dramatic masterpiece"—

matched in cosmic importance, presumably, only by the better works of W. Shakespeare.

One reason for this unanimous accolade is that *Cavalcade* is a "good" movie. The other, and more obvious, reason is that Noel Coward, a very shrewd man, wrote a shrewd patriotic spectacle, and if there is anything that moves the ordinary American to uncontrollable tears, it is the plight—the constant plight—of dear old England.

In picture form, *Cavalcade* is a superlative newsreel, forcibly strengthened by factual scenes, good music, and wonderful photography. It is marred by pat and obvious dramatic climaxes, and by a conclusion which is anticlimactical and meaningless. And when one forgets the pace, the flow, and the really dignified and lovely quality of the picture—which is easier said than done—one can hear some very cheap theatrical observations from the choleric old empire-builder, Mr. Coward.

There was many a sob in the audience during the charming scene which dramatized the funeral of the great queen, Victoria. But why? The scene itself reached no dramatic ceiling. And it was not a tragic death. I do not want indirectly to deprecate a fine production with a speech (which I am ready to deliver at the drop of a hat) on the silly deference most of our writing boys show visiting Englishmen, and I mention the sobs attending this one scene in the movie as an indication of the fact that, while the audience was moved, Hollywood, and the cast and crew hired out there, deserved no little credit for it.

The music, and the extraordinary pictorial dignity, made death itself dramatic; the scene gave one a melancholy, impressionistic feeling of the passing of all things. And this same fine work on the part of Director Frank Lloyd and his assistant, William Cameron Menzies, made the war scenes equally as impressive, even though one could not help but remember that the brave laddies who relieved Mafeking were engaging in one of the most ignominious wars England ever waged.

As far as the subject matter was concerned, I personally enjoyed the scene in *The Wet Parade* of a Tammany celebration in 1912 more than any of the chapters of English history dramatized in

Mr. Coward's spectacle. Yet seldom has a movie company released a finer technical production than *Cavalcade*, and Mr. Lloyd—who once did a charming and unusual and really legitimate movie called *Young Nowheres*—and Mr. Menzies—who, since the beginning of Hollywood, has been the one man in the business who has brought imagination, skill, and a sense of beauty to the most neglected department in the industry, scenic designing—deserve the highest praise for their work.

Mr. Lloyd might have spared us the brokenhearted mother waving her little flag Armistice night, and he might have aided Mr. Coward if he had put the tinkly song, "Twentieth Century Blues," in an earlier section of the picture. Furthermore, he might have greatly aided Mr. Coward if he had cut a shoddy bit of theatrical nobility and denied us the sophomoric toast, given in conclusion by the old father and mother, in which they hope "grace and dignity and peace" may be restored to old England. I can repeat, but not print, what the shade of Ben Jonson and his boys must have said to that.

As for Mr. Menzies, I don't think his work could have been improved upon. If you remember *The Thief of Bagdad, Robin Hood,* and *Bulldog Drummond*, you may recall that the sets were half the shows. Mr. Menzies made them, and I hope he makes many more.

I have one more complaint to register and then you can go and cry your eyes out at the sight of "the march of time measured by a human heart—a mother's heart." (Advt.) Ursula Jeans, especially imported from London for *Cavalcade*, was cold and unattractive. With the aid of a good hairdresser, a modiste, and a George Kaufman to direct her, she might be able to compete with any one of the other forty young actresses already sold down the river to Hollywood.

Vanity Fair, March, 1933

SHE DONE HIM WRONG

Sᴇx ʜᴀs not entirely disappeared from the screen, but like the horse in transportation it is a minor necessity in the movie industry these days. An old-fashioned reactionary myself, I must say that I find the new fashion in picture plots a mixed blessing, and it was a pleasant surprise to discover Mae West, swan bed and all, in a movie version of her great play, "Diamond Lil."

With less care, the whole production might have become one of those *For Men Only* jobs, or worse yet, it might have been one of those self-conscious satires on the Gay Nineties—one of those dull plays in which even the extras think themselves too, too funny in make-up, and consequently go about giggling with uncontrollable laughter at the whole thing.

She Done Him Wrong is played straight and to the hilt, and as a result it is good fun. Miss West sings "Easy Rider," "I Like a Slow Man," and "Frankie and Johnny" as though Stanford White and Harry K. Thaw really were sitting in the front row. John Bright kept a good melodramatic pace in the manuscript. The production itself is surprisingly good; the sets and lighting, and the general direction, handled by Lowell Sherman, are way above par.

What most producers will fail to understand is that this picture is not just smutty, and that, although definitely a burlesque show, it has a certain beery poignancy and, above all, a gusto about it which makes it a good show.

Vanity Fair, March, 1933

STATE FAIR

A ᴘᴜɴɢᴇɴᴛ, good-humored novel of Ioway, called "State Fair," has been turned, almost miraculously, into a good-humored, pungent motion picture. The director, Henry King, has told a good story well; he has ably characterized some yeomen from the empire

of tall corn; he has used music better than most American directors; and he has made even Janet Gaynor fairly human at times.

The novel itself could have been used by Mr. King to make a
distinguished esoteric name for himself if he had wanted to go to
the trouble. It takes a wealthy farmer, his wife, and their two children to the state fair, and allows the children to have their first
love affairs while the farmer is winning a prize for his Hampshire
boar and his wife is triumphing in the mince-meat arena.

When I saw how well Mr. King was doing the job, I began to
wish he had designed his picture after *Sunrise*, and had given us an
impressionistic, kaleidoscopic, musical melodrama, rather than a
straight narrative; but for years I have been lamenting the lack of
Americana in motion picture plots, and now that I find genuine
farm people on the screen I'm not going to complain.

Among the many pleasant surprises in this movie is that ubiqui-
tous, homespun humorist, Will Rogers. For the first time since his
silent picture days, Mr. Rogers is made to act and not comment.
He plays stooge to a champion hog called Blue Boy, and he does it
with a great deal of skill. Not once does he step forth to mention
Hoover, Mussolini, or any of his autograph-signers. And, forced to
go to work, he becomes a top-notch actor and comedian. What
humor Mr. Rogers engages in is to the point, a fact which may be
explained by the vague presence of Frank Craven in and out of the
picture, and, also, by the fact that Paul Green had something to
do with the scenario.

The bit parts—such as the professors from Ames who judge the
hogs and the carnival barkers—are all well done. Louise Dresser,
Lew Ayres, Norman Foster, and Sally Eilers seem, under Mr. King's
supervision, far better than usual and, although at times you may
want to kick her squarely in the teeth, Janet Gaynor becomes under the same gifted hand almost as winsome as she earnestly sets
out to be.

I congratulate Mr. King, Mr. Rogers, Mr. Craven, Mr. Green,
Iowa, and Blue Boy. *State Fair* is a good job.

Vanity Fair, March, 1933

M

ORDINARILY, I do not like to waste space writing about the significance of foreign pictures. We get no more interesting pictures from Europe than we do from Hollywood, and along with these we get as much horrible junk as was ever turned out by any local company. But most moviegoers probably have the notion that, somehow or other, those fellows over there certainly have it all over us when it comes to making pictures.

Actually, you can look at a hundred German pictures, and you'll find that a majority of the directors are patently imitating Hollywood. And while the Russians have had a world at the service of their cameras, the sum total of their good productions can be added on one hand.

There are two or three men in Russia, one in France, one in England, a half dozen in Germany, and about four in Hollywood who have conceived and executed some originality in motion pictures, but even that originality has been more literary than technical; that is, where Pudovkin, or Murnau, or Chaplin may have designed a camera trick or a cutting trick any good director immediately could seize upon, it is only when an educated man uses such skill to turn a personal, literary idea into a movie that we have that rare thing, a fine movie. Thus, it is not so much technical originality, but René Clair, that made A Nous la Liberté good; Murnau, and not Flaherty's photography, that made Tabu a lovely thing; it is Fritz Lang, and not "the Germans," who is responsible for a picture, long famous in Europe and Hollywood, called M— a movie which already has greatly influenced good directors, and which, along with its esoteric technical innovations, also is a beautifully balanced melodrama, well worth space in any language.

M is the story of a sex murderer (apprehended some years ago) known as the "Düsseldorf Murderer." Lang immediately has a cultural advantage over local contemporaries, both in his understanding of the character and in his audiences. Knowing him only as a "fiend slayer," few local audiences will find anything in this murderer that will agree with their impressions of how a fiend slayer feels, or how he acts. I imagine that's why the censors let it through; looking for bloody gangster monkeyshines, they found only a pudgy, pop-eyed, simple-faced young German with a puzzling predilection for little girls. With the exception of one scene in which he displays a spring knife, there is no obvious indication of crime or sex in the picture. There is one scene in which he is frustrated, and collapses in a café—and another in which he confesses and reenacts his crimes—that is tragically real, and, to a civilized person, about as horrible as anything you ever want to see.

The photography is straightforward and austere. There is no acting in the picture. Every character, from the murderer to the most insignificant extra, is beaten into subordination. You feel as though you were watching a newsreel. Never for an instant do you say, "Ah, what an actor!" There are no camera angles, no whirling cogs, no Coney Island tricks with faces thrown out of focus.

This newsreel quality of M does force an admission that some Germans and Russians are able to get an unusual quality into even mediocre pictures, such as Comradeship. That quality is subordination. A German director, now in Hollywood, was talking last winter about the amazing use of dialogue in M, and how Lang puts the audience right into his scenes by never showing the speaker— or by thrusting his camera into a group of people and making them so absolutely natural that the audience feels that it, too, is actually seeing and hearing with the cast. We agreed that you could not make such a picture in Hollywood, even if the producers kept their hands off the production, simply because in all America you could hardly collect a hundred actors and put them in a picture and keep them from acting. In a job such as I Am a Fugitive, every man and woman within a hundred yards of camera range is acting his head off, figuring that he is a Clark Gable or a Garbo, as the case may be, who needs only to project himself strongly enough to have the director send post-haste for him to sign that big contract.

This is not just a Hollywood characteristic, although it is the main reason why Clair and Lang and Pabst can make pictures which ring absolutely true and which are so convincing that one forgets one is seeing a dramatic production, while our best productions are obvious and theatrical. As a friend pointed out, it is true of most American art. He directed a successful show some years ago, and spoke about his troubles with the cast. "They have no humility." A crackpot theatrical producer, given a fragile little comedy, rehearses his cast with all the temperament and unreasonable tyranny of a Stanislavski producing "The Seagull." The author of a successful puzzle book overnight assumes alcoholic temperament that would shame a Hearn or an Oscar Wilde. The play, the job itself, is never the thing.

Even when Hollywood does go, we won't be able to make an M unless independent companies allow their directors to do away entirely with actors, and (which is the only sensible way to manufacture movies at all) pick types and faces off the street.

Meanwhile, until the millennium, Hollywood's poverty has been a minor blessing. Starved for pictures, theatre owners will show anything, and we can expect to see the best things the Russians, the Chinese, the Irish, and the Fiji Islanders have to show us—a condition impossible in the good old blackjack corporation days.

Vanity Fair, May, 1933

GABRIEL OVER THE WHITE HOUSE

As was true of *Washington Merry-Go-Round*, *Washington Masquerade* and *I Am a Fugitive*, *Gabriel Over the White House* is not an exciting picture because of skillful dramaturgy, but because of the very contemporary, dramatic subject of the picture itself.

This picture had to be cut because of political pressure, with the result that the concluding scenes are rather lame. In the original print, a typical Warren Gamaliel Harding is put into the White House by a typical Ohio gang. During the first days of office, he hands out ambassadorships and appointments with good Republican carelessness, although an army of unemployed is encamped in Central Park, threatening to march on Washington.

Walter Huston, as the President, drives his car over an embankment and has concussion of the brain. Presumably divine power brings him to life; he begins to study the conditions of the country and, much to the horror of his cohorts, gradually wins such popular support that he is made a dictator. It is during these scenes that you may find yourself becoming shamefully, un-Americanly patriotic; when Huston arrives in Baltimore and announces to an army of men that it seems to him undignified for a President's people to walk to him on tired feet—that the least he could do was to meet them—you may recollect a miraculously distant year when the Chief of Staff of the Army actually was called upon to move tanks, artillery, cavalry, and infantry upon a body of unarmed, if misled, ex-soldiers.

Strangely enough—although you may never have found it in our fast-yellowing press—the President of *Gabriel Over the White House* forms an enlisted army of unemployed, subject to mitigated military discipline—a fiction which Roosevelt already has made a fact.

In the anonymously written novel there was an exciting war, which was originally included in the movie. This war was finally deleted from the picture, probably at the request of a new State Department. The movie now ends with a pointless peace conference, whereas it originally had some exciting and pleasant scenes showing an Anglo Saxon Navy blowing the Japanese Islands out of the Pacific. (Note to the editor: I'm not trying to get an offer from Hearst—I merely think as long as we are heading for war, it would be pleasant to have the Navy do all the work, seeing as how it hasn't been in a battle since Perry barged around the Great Lakes.)

Walter Huston has a recitative monotony which I dislike, but he makes his President dignified enough to make this one-man picture plausible. The gangster killings could have been done with less exaggeration, but the marching army, the one speech in the Senate in which Huston offers to put the country under martial law, and the veracity of the incidents themselves make *Gabriel Over the White House* what the press would call a "stirring" movie.

Judge, May 20, 1933

DEVIL'S BROTHER

WHAT should have been the most interesting picture of the year has turned out to be an uneven slapstick comedy, with musical sequences which, unfortunately, are so poorly done that they seem oddly unrelated to the antics of the leading men, Laurel and Hardy.

Whoever chose Auber's light opera, "Fra Diavolo," as the basis of a story for Laurel and Hardy certainly had a shrewd idea. Stan Laurel, with his vacuous stare, his lantern jaw, and his gigantic complacency, is a perfect Bottom the Weaver and, more than almost any actor they might have chosen, he breaks down the feeling of artificiality you almost inevitably get when you spy a group of actors dressed in wigs and short trousers.

They could hardly have chosen a better light opera lead than Dennis King; at least, I know of none who is less offensive when called upon to make love in E-flat. With a rather unusual idea, with two comics who fit into the atmosphere as well as into the libretto of an eighteenth century operetta, and with a handsome and able fellow to do their singing—here was an idea a little beyond the boundary of Hollywood's story pasture.

As it happens only too often, however, the director failed to show any selective judgment. His comics made up for the long stretches of narrative stupidity in the original libretto by indulging in some of their first-rate music hall pantomime. This should have been enough, but the director did not cut the arch comedy that goes on between the bold bandits and the loose lady of fashion; it throws the whole show out of key. He eliminated almost all the music, but his remaining choruses were handled abominably. His sets, his groups, his costumes, his sound—everything connected with the singing, in other words—is poor, and seems to have no connection with Laurel and Hardy, or the well-worn but still entertaining plot.

Above all, he didn't keep the thing moving, certainly a prime requisite in comedy. He dragged out the scenes in milady's boudoir, with Thelma Todd—usually stooge for the Marx Brothers —burlesquing a characterization which, if done at all, certainly should have been played straight.

Yet, for all its lame direction, *Devil's Brother* is an encouraging picture. It is funny enough, and simple enough, to amuse you; more important, it is in the tradition of old-time movie comedy, of the stuff we used to get from Chaplin and Fairbanks. Movies are better than they were in those days. Music cannot be handled so loosely when we have had *Le Million* and *42nd Street* for classroom consideration. But if we are to have a musical revival in pictures, the general idea of *Devil's Brother* points the most satisfactory way. The old light operas allow farce and burlesque, they have good music, and they can be set in a realm of nonesuch, which is real movie territory, made for the camera.

Vanity Fair, August, 1933

THE AMATEURS

THERE isn't a barn or a county seat in the length and breadth of the land that hasn't its group of amateur players working blithely away in a heady atmosphere of pure Art for what they erroneously hope will be the greater glory of the drama; and, if nothing else, these amateur companies have at least furnished a refuge for disappointed trombone players, discharged sign painters, and disgraced choir leaders who might otherwise clutter up the ordinary channels of society.

One doesn't need to look any further, however, than the lists of plays annually produced by these people, for proof that the only aid they give the theatre by their meretricious reproductions of popular hits of yesterday, is to drive customers to Broadway and the movie theatre.

These would-be actors and producers (who are not to be confused with the established players who take their art to green pastures or sand dunes for a summer vacation) are dismally unsuccessful because they are quite blissfully unaware of what the theatre is all about. They try to substitute a sort of vague idealism and arty temperament for the long and difficult technical training that is the essential foundation of a skillfully smooth dramatic performance. The result is inevitably appalling and embarrassing to all present—a disjointed, false, uncomfortable nightmare, reminiscent of parents' night at the local high school.

On the other hand, a moving picture camera is more nearly foolproof than the legitimate stage, and for this reason promises infinitely more happy results to the amateur, if he will give only a modicum of thought and imagination to its use. A camera cannot indulge in temperamental acrobatics; it can be carted anywhere, and all the amateur producer needs is a professional cameraman, an idea, and five thousand dollars' worth of equipment in order to make a good picture. Furthermore, the amateur, with the slightest degree of imagination and just a mediocre assistant, has the opportunity to make with his own hands a meritorious piece of work simply because he has so many fresh locales, so many new subjects to work with, that are avoided by the Hollywood producers. And certainly he doesn't have to cope with the stagehands' union, the costumer, the box-office men, the receiver's lawyer for the theatre, and all the other tribulations that beset the path of the amateur producer who attempts to crash Broadway and finds that, for all he has to do with the creation of a play, he might just as well be endorsing checks and sending them to Moosehart.

A few young men have made pictures on their own and those I have seen have been worth the trouble. Young Frissell, who died tragically on an expedition to improve his picture, went to Newfoundland with Captain Bob Bartlett and George Melford (the old-time director who made *The Sheik*) and made a fine dramatization of the seal fishermen which, even in its unfinished state, was exciting and well-photographed. Douglas Burden made even a better and more polished dramatization of the Ojibway Indians.

While they lacked story and form, the round-the-world pictures taken by W. K. Vanderbilt had a nice clarity and a newsreel interest that made them the equal of a dozen Hollywood-financed travel pictures. And, before he became a Great Executive, Merian

Cooper made *Grass*, which still rates as one of the best movies we have ever made. Yet, with these examples before them, few amateurs show any interest in the camera.

Judging from those I have run across, the curse of the amateur is his sordid commercialism. If there is one thing your ambitious amateur abhors above all else, it is the thought that he might be accused of being "arty," or even slightly interested in improving the standard of an art. "Of course," he will hasten to explain to you, "I don't care whether you like the idea or not, or whether it is any good—I just want to make money."

(Evidently the only people dabbling with movies and the theatre—with the rare exceptions noted—who carelessly gamble thousands for a Hemingway or a Somerset Maugham, are the Adolph Zukors, Winnie Sheehans, and the Sam Harrises.)

A standard feature movie costs a deal of real money, no matter how economically it is produced. The equipment and the costs of production to an amateur are almost prohibitive, even though they should run a third below the average cost of a Hollywood picture (which is, roughly, a quarter of a million dollars and sometimes runs well over this).

This item possibly has frightened off ambitious movie producers with original ideas and a genuine desire to make good pictures—but I doubt it. You have only to consider the small movie camera to find the answer as to why, in a country where a hundred million admissions are paid into movie theatres, practically no one has had the imagination, skill, or ambition to make a picture for fun.

There are, by the last figures I saw, over a hundred thousand small movie cameras in this country; there are some two hundred clubs whose members make amateur movies. And the net result, gentlemen, is seven hundred thousand, two hundred and fifty pictures a month showing Aunt Grace dimly walking across the lawn; plus nine hundred and fifteen thousand, two hundred and twenty movies showing Junior glaring at the birdy.

Here, then, are a few simple reasons why we have no good small movies—and, believe me, when I say they're no good, I mean they are appalling: first, because the ordinary camera owner has no understanding of the fundamental principles of moviemaking; and second, because he is so muscle-bound he would rather have Holly-wood make his pictures, radio give him his music, and the press his literature, than make something himself.

Like all amateurs, those who really try to make movies make the fatal error of trying to be "different" before they even learn the first principles of their craft. The amateur doesn't even learn how to focus his camera. And he has absolutely no regard for light or shade—or even simple, clear pictures. The amateurs use their movie cameras like a still camera—they never associate their own work with, for instance, the work of Lee Garmes in such things as *Shanghai Express* and *Zoo in Budapest*. And they make the same mistakes as the professionals—only more so.

Vanity Fair, August, 1933

THUNDER OVER MEXICO

W HEN Paramount wouldn't let him make a movie, Eisenstein went to Mexico with $75,000 of Upton Sinclair's money and made 200,000 feet of film. Hollywood has never heard of Mexico —because Mexico has never been on Broadway, and Sam Harris and George Kaufman have never done anything about Mexico. Even so, they might examine the seven thousand feet of *Thunder Over Mexico* which Upton Sinclair has released.

Here, gentlemen, are pictures. Infinite variety of light and shadow, poised dignity in close-ups which move the emotions faster than an act of dialogue, but pictures, pictures—beautiful, skillful, exciting, and real. As you are in the picture business, gen-tlemen, *Thunder Over Mexico* might be of interest to you.

I won't attempt to discuss this silent movie in the terminology of the Communist, or camp-meeting, critical school, simply be-cause I don't understand it. Eisenstein has a fine knowledge of the mechanics of the camera, and with that he has a picture mind and picture sense. Whatever he is attempting to say, he articulates only in photography. Mr. Cukor may not have heard about it, but this is an exciting business. Where a playwright makes a new draft of a scene, Eisenstein cuts a sequence of pictures and interpolates another set of portraits. You can call this "montage in hierogly-phics," or whatever you like. I call it movie-making.

There is a distinct and individual tempo to a movie made as it should be. Your reactions are slower, and while your attention is as concentrated, you wait for the pictures to speak—you ponder over them—you relax far more than you can when you have to listen as well as see. This is true of talking movies as they are made by Lang and René Clair—in *M* or *Sous les Toits de Paris*. While the emotional impact is as strong as it is in the theatre, the char-acters on the screen seem suspended in a charming vista; all mo-tion, all thought seem slower and more graceful, as they appear to a heroin addict.

Of course, Eisenstein is blunt, exaggerated, and naive in his story-telling. The workers are always right, the employers always wrong. Yet he gets a religious quality in his characters, because he surrounds them with beauty and dignity; he chooses them for their native grace, and you cannot say that his distorted story-tell-ing is dull, for all its overemphasis.

The simple plot in this small portion of his gigantic movie con-cerns a peon girl who is raped by a guard, which results in an abor-tive revolt which is cruelly suppressed. Aroused by this last act of cruelty, the workers revolt, and everything is hotsy-totsy after the revolution is won.

I can't join with the camp-meeting boys and wail about the fact that Eisenstein didn't cut the few thousand feet of film in *Thun-der Over Mexico*. If he had, the story probably would have lost in over-exaggeration what it gained in technical excellence. I doubt, too, that he would have cut it under twenty thousand feet. What-ever he chose from a day's sitting of movie would have been frag-mentary. The fragment we have is enough to make you see and feel Mexico; it is lovely, and it takes you far enough West of Broadway to be extraordinarily novel.

I am inclined to believe Upton Sinclair's statement that Eisen-stein fell in love with Mexico and would have stayed there if Mex-ico, the United States, and his own country hadn't all objected to it. Certainly there is a devotional quality in the picture which transcends anything to be found in *Old and New* or any of the other Eisenstein pictures.

However, I am highly uninterested in the controversy over the genesis of *Thunder Over Mexico*; I don't care whether Upton Sinclair stole the movie from Eisenstein, or whether Eisenstein _an out with some Pasadena money, or whether the seven thousand feet of film cut from the picture is the least important of the story sequences in the whole film.

It does interest me, however, that these independent productions, the foreign pictures and the sidelines of the movies, the travel, adventure, and newsreel productions, are improving and becoming more popular, while Hollywood gets closer and closer to Broadway and farther and farther from the legitimate form of the movie. All of which indicates that the day is not far off when the independent director, working with independent money, will soon make the only movies we have, while the producers who are so frantically mating with a moribund Broadway will find themselves up a blind alley, their pockets emptied.

Vanity Fair, October, 1933

DINNER AT EIGHT

Y OU MAY have heard that Metro-Goldwyn-Mayer paid over $100,000 for the Kaufman-Ferber play, "Dinner at Eight"; that they employed Frances Marion, Herman Mankiewicz, and Donald Ogden Stewart to rewrite it, and George Cukor to direct a group of famous people: John and Lionel Barrymore, Marie Dressler, Lee Tracy, Jean Harlow, Billie Burke, Wallace Beery, Louise Closser Hale, and Madge Evans. All this sounds expensive and impressive. Seldom, gentlemen, have you ever seen such a glittering galaxy of stars!—wealth!—talent!—and sheer brute force gathered together under one tent. So let us approach this great exhibition with proper awe and care.

Mr. Cukor and his supervisor, Mr. Selznick, had an expensive and successful play on their hands. The form of the play presented a difficult problem of direction. Like "Grand Hotel," the novelty and pace of "Dinner at Eight" accounted for part of its success. Both really are more movies than plays. Using a revolving stage, Mr. Kaufman, with his usual precise, machine-like direction, presented an amazing number of scenes, in which the customers saw thumbnail dramas in the lives of six couples, at a smooth, swift pace—so effortless and swift that the characters seemed almost like people in a newsreel.

Now this kaleidoscopic, cross-section method of story-telling is novel on the stage. It is the very basic principle, however, of movie-making. The camera can go anywhere. What is a tough assignment for a crew of stagehands is child's play in the hands of a third assistant cameraman.

What Mr. Cukor had was an old-fashioned movie scenario on his hands. Yet he chose (wisely, considering his unexciting record) to take no chances with directorial experimentation. He set up his camera on a stage, and photographed *Dinner at Eight* just exactly as it appeared in the Music Box Theatre last year. You will get no atmospheric camera studies, no photomontage, no music, no outdoor scenes in this picture.

Of course, you cannot focus a camera on a stage from what would be thirteenth row center and register as much as your eyes naturally encompass. It was necessary, then, to freeze the movie characters in their important scenes and show close-up shots of them delivering their lines. This, unfortunately, slows down the pace of the picture, and you'll find a paradox in *Dinner at Eight* (one based on sheer mechanics): a dramatization moving slower on the screen—where it can be put together in a laboratory—than it did on the stage.

But now that you have some idea of the difficult form of the play, and the successful manner in which Mr. Cukor and Mr. Selznick worked that out, hold tight, and we'll take a look at the content of this million-dollar movie manuscript.

The characters of the play include a Mr. and Mrs. Oliver Jordan of Park Avenue, who are giving a dinner, and their prospective guests. These guests are: Dan Packard, a self-made crooked promoter, and his chippie wife; a broken-down movie actor who has seduced the nineteen-year-old daughter of the hostess; a passé but internationally known theatrical demi-mondaine; a doctor—who is sleeping with Mrs. Packard—and his broken-hearted wife; the Jordan girl's fiancé, Ernest; and two poor relatives who are invited to dinner at the last minute.

The scenario writers barely touched the manuscript. They deleted two lines from Carlotta Vance's entrance scene, which were only two of the funniest lines in the show; they added a few sympathetic servants; they completely rewrote the concluding scene. They did eliminate the kitchen scenes, but nowhere does the writing help Mr. Cukor get any movement into his people.

As Mr. Jordan, his wife, the doctor and his wife, the movie actor, the actress—in fact, all but three of the characters—are dying (are, dramatically, dead—defeated, embittered people), the slow picturization of their disinterment makes you ill at ease. You begin to fidget, look at your watch and calculate how long it will take the chauffeur to drive home from the cemetery.

Lee Tracy, as a sincere, patient little Broadway agent, and Jean Harlow and Wallace Beery, as a pair of gutter buckaroos, have life and blood in them, and they are splendid.

As for the others, they are all first-rate, but wherever, as with Lionel Barrymore, they bring charm or kindliness to their people, they are merely fighting the playwrights, struggling against writing which called for neither quality.

Mr. Kaufman and Miss Ferber were consistent. They left their characters at the end of the play barely suspended over their open graves, but the scenario writers miraculously shoot adrenalin into their stiffs at the last moment. The empty-headed Mrs. Jordan becomes a loving wife; the promoter's fish-wife saves the Jordan shipping line from her husband's crooked machinations; the deflowered debutante looks forward to a pleasant wedding—and instead of turning on the audience with a surly sneer, the whole dinner party startlingly smile through their tears as they go in to eat.

This universal amnesty merely refutes everything that went on in the play. Where the dinner guests were shallow, cheap, and sordid, they suddenly become like Miss Ferber's Woman's Home Companion heroines; they become not only highly unimportant, but completely unreal.

I suppose *Dinner at Eight* will be regarded as a magnificent movie production, skillfully played by a troupe of famous movie stars, by a press and public which regards a picture as a stage play put on celluloid. *Dinner at Eight* remains, nevertheless, a fearful re-creation of a play which had nothing to recommend itself in the first place except two heretofore able authors, a brilliant director, a wise producer, incredible ballyhoo, and a successful run.

Vanity Fair, October, 1933

A DEPOSED EMPEROR

THOSE of you who ever sat in the drafty pews of the old Province-town Theatre and were almost blown out of your uncomfortable seats by the tom-tomming that turned Emperor Jones into a gibbering idiot, probably anticipated, as I certainly did, something exciting from Paul Robeson in the movie version of the O'Neill play.

I had a genuine feeling of anticipation before I went to see the picture, because it was produced under what were, if there is such a thing in the theatre, ideal conditions.

Two young producers bought the play and made it in the old Paramount studios on Long Island. Thus, whatever mistakes they might naturally make, one felt that we would be spared typical Hollywood errors: a mulatto chorus routine in the Emperor's palace, or, as conceivable, Johnny Mack Brown or Clark Gable in blackface, cast in the role of Brutus Jones.

The director they hired, Dudley Murphy, has long agitated independent ideas in movie circles, although he has only Hollywood pot-boilers and a three-reel curio, made years ago, to his credit. Yet here was a director with ideas; a famous manuscript; a natural choice for the lead, Paul Robeson—who already had done the part to great acclaim in London and in New York; a tried author, Du Bose Heyward, to work on the scenario; and a general freedom from the salesmen, bankers, vice-presidents, and supervisors who invariably smear their hands over the best celluloid Hollywood produces.

The result, to my amazement, was an unexciting and indifferent motion picture. A snap judgment would indict Du Bose Heyward and Director Murphy for all the shortcomings in the production. In order to make a full-length picture, the scenario writer took the early incidents in the life of Brutus Jones, and carefully, if prosaically, wrote them into a preface to the original play. O'Neill indicated the Pullman porter's past by a few paragraphs of dialogue; in the picture, we began with a stagey revival meeting that seems to be part of last season's Hall Johnson Negro show, *Run Little Chillun*; and at the very start, Brutus Jones seems a great deal more superficial than O'Neill's Emperor.

From his hometown, Heyward took Jones to Harlem, and here again Director Murphy showed his provincialism by having his Pullman porter hero dining and dancing in the Cotton Club, a proceeding as phony-looking as it was implausible. Throughout these scenes, Brutus Jones becomes merely a brash rooster of a Negro, taking his fun where he finds it and boasting as he goes.

There is an incredible scene in the President's private car and then, finally, for the first time, we have a legitimate bit of drama, when Brutus kills his friend, Jeff, in a quarrel following a crap game. This is also the first sequence that has any bearing on the incidents in the original play.

The subsequent chain gang shots, the escape, and Jones' usurpation of the throne of a tiny kingdom, seem more like a part of a Gus Hill olio routine than a melodrama; not so much because of actual comic writing, but because none of the people appear real or important to Brutus Jones, so that his strutting and boasting seem so many unanswered cues for the interlocutor.

This indifferent writing and worse direction was a matter of judgment. The eight-scene play would have made only three reels of film at the most; they had to lengthen the show some way in order to make a major production of it. They took the most cautious ways and then didn't do justice to their work.

However, once they get Brutus Jones on the throne, the Messrs. Heyward and Murphy never once maltreat a line or situation, and the original play comes tagging along, completely intact, behind this hodge-podge preface.

Without going into technical details, the timing and sound of the drum and the dissolves in which Jones sees his past, in drum tempo, rising around him in the forest, are far below the photographic standard one may find in any humdrum Hollywood movie, and for two reasons: the Astoria equipment is old-fashioned, and so is Mr. Murphy.

Yet, while mistakes in judgment and lack of technical skill emasculated the picture to some extent, this doesn't explain why, in the closing scenes, Emperor Jones still remained unexciting. After all, it has not been many years since a Negro movie would have been banned entirely from the screen by Elder Hays. We seldom have a picture which has a direct emotional dramatic situation without Janet Gaynor or Constance Bennett or some other queen stepping bang into the show, making it just another movie. And Emperor Jones is not that.

So, after blaming the director and author completely, I suddenly realized that Paul Robeson, a fine figure of a man and a singer who is completely satisfying, is equally culpable.

He has two faults that make his Emperor a wax figure and not a living, fearful man. One is his self-conscious acting; the other, a similar fault, is the over-broad gestures, grimaces, and surface emotional show peculiar to concert singers who have to portray a regiment of soldiers charging a castle wall and keep in tune at the same time.

There are few times one has any undue excitement in this business, and I was not only disappointed in *Emperor Jones*, but genuinely sorry the show didn't come off. While I have no particular interest in the finances of Krimsky and Cochran, they can completely bowl over the inbred producing system in Hollywood by making courageous independent pictures, and, indifferent as it is, I hope they make a profit from the production—they're on the right track.

I have a feeling that today the play itself couldn't be exciting in anything but a drafty little theatre. It is not a full-fledged show; it is O'Neill of thirteen years ago, and it can't be stretched any further than the narrow limits of the Provincetown stage. It hasn't the poetry or the stride of the later O'Neill plays. It is a fugue for drum and actor, and the drum is in no way as exciting as it was in 1920.

Vanity Fair, November, 1933

NIGHT FLIGHT

A s a production, I have seldom seen a more earnest adaptation than *Night Flight*. It was an unusual, elusive bit of writing they had to deal with. The one crescendo of the story is splendidly handled—the scene in which the Aeropostale pilot climbs over a cyclone and flies in a peaceful, moon-lit sky until his gas tank is empty and he crashes. Most of it was made out of doors and not in the studio—a much more difficult bit of work than the film shows.

Yet it is astonishing that one crew of people could photograph an impressionistic story like *Night Flight* so successfully, and then let their own production down with a rodeo publicity stunt.

Here was a motion picture dealing with flying and the feeling of flying. As in the novel, the fliers became robots; nature and the machinery were the players. Having given us this feeling, didn't they turn around and bill the show as another salary fest, with Helen Hayes, Clark Gable, some of the Barrymores, Robert Montgomery, and Myrna Loy offered as the main attractions? Asked to watch these famous fellows do their tricks, the customers naturally felt cheated, because the players were subordinate to the production; the fine atmosphere and flavor of the show were lost for a few scenes of wretched emoting.

If John Barrymore hadn't chosen this particular picture in which to loaf, *Night Flight* might have had a consistent feeling in it; but

Mr. Barrymore growled where he should have whispered; where he was supposed to be a high-strung, self-possessed, and weary man, he clenched his fists and glowered and yelled and mumbled, and put on, in general, as terrible an exhibition of gas-light acting as I've ever seen in my life.

With an anonymous cast, *Night Flight* would have been the most legitimate and exciting job of the year. With a highly-publicized cast it was spotty and misunderstood.

Vanity Fair, December, 1933

THE PRIVATE LIFE OF HENRY THE EIGHTH

The Private Life of Henry the Eighth is a comedy that is a comedy. In view of the delicacy that hangs like a gentle perfume over the collected works of almost all post-war English writers, it is difficult to believe that a crew of young Englishmen could manufacture a comedy about an English king that would not at some point or other get up on its toes and dance lightly out of the bounds of Elizabethan humor to the tune of "Poor Little Rich Girl" or "Twentieth Century Blues." Lacking this almost inevitable violet taint, it is only natural to presume that, in accord with the tradition of almost any historical play you care to mention, the comedy should be a matter of broad allusion to known historical fact, the sentiment a matter of pontifical utterance rewritten from the nearest grammar-school history.

Then, too, you expect to be taken into the author's confidence, as in *Berkeley Square*, and allowed to laugh with him at the funny clothes, the odd manners, and the vulgarities of another day.

It took a high order of intelligence to write the scenario for *The Private Life of Henry the Eighth*, to make it believable, moving, amusing, and yet to escape the pitfalls of historical dramatization we have listed.

Not only was this accomplished splendidly, but Alexander Korda, a Hollywood expatriate, gave the picture a good photo-

graphic flavor. Above all, he directed his mob scenes with a knowing hand, so that, perhaps for the first time, a group of actors in
costume really look as though they were eating, drinking, and living people, and not so many extras chewing gum and squirming
under their greasepaint.

Unless you care to do a little research on the subject, you will
not appreciate how difficult it must have been for an Englishman
to write about England and still not sound like a half-soused rural
Fourth of July orator (*vide* the last scene in *Cavalcade*).

But there is more to *The Private Life of Henry the Eighth* than
a merit of omissions and selection; there is an uproarious, highly
intelligent, and completely satisfying performance by Charles
Laughton, who would have been worth seeing in a mediocre picture, but who had around him a very good crew, and a general
production unlike anything ever made in England in the way of
a motion picture.

Vanity Fair, December, 1933

THE INFORMER

IT HAS been a constant paradox of movie-making that the most
memorable productions of all time have made actors and actresses famous, while famous actors and actresses seldom appear
in movies of more than passing importance, simply because all
logic, balance, and drama in a "star" picture are thrown aside in
order that the one personality may be blown to the skies.

The best picture of the season to date is *The Informer*, a terse,
brutal story of the Irish revolution—a sombre portrait of a rabbit-
minded giant who betrays his best friend and is hunted to his
doom against the leaden background of war-torn Dublin.

Because of the scenario, the direction, lighting and the balance
of the picture, Victor McLaglen, who plays the lead, probably will
be considered a great actor, yet he obviously is no such thing because in fifty previous second-rate movies he has shown nothing

more brilliant than a hearty personality and a handsome set of teeth.

McCall's, August, 1935

THE 39 STEPS

IT LONG has been a theatrical tradition that as soon as dog days set in the entire country suffers a mental collapse, during which period even a Brain Truster finds it impossible to count above ten, read anything more erudite than the baseball scores, or discuss anything more profound than the weather. As a result, most theatres are now exhibiting childish adventure or mystery tales, such as *Unknown Woman, Charlie Chan in Egypt, The Secret Agent, The Great Scotland Yard Mystery, The Clairvoyant, She, Front Page Woman*, and *The Raven*. The general fault in these productions is that the producers not only have made their hot-weather fare simple, but have put no care or thought into their material.

There is one fine exception to this hot-weather rule of mediocrity—a picture called *The 39 Steps*. Written by the distinguished Scot now Governor-General of Canada, John Buchan, the picture is well played, skillfully directed, beautifully photographed, and is in every way the best production of the month.

The picture starts as any salty adventure tale should, with a "Bang! Bang! and two Indians bit the dust," when an amiable young man rescues a strange woman from a music hall riot, only to have her fall murdered over his bed an hour later. All he has learned in the meantime is that the woman is a spy and that by rescuing her he himself became suspect, which means that for the duration of his exciting adventures he is sought as a murderer by the police and as a dangerous agent by a syndicate of spies.

The real virtue of the picture, above all else, is in the neat story design; scene leads into scene easily and smoothly, and there are at least two climaxes which will bring you up sharp in your seat. And, just because it deals with spies, don't think *The 39 Steps* has much to do with spying. The hero at no time has any idea where his spies are or what they look like, and for the most part concerns himself with trying to get away from a young lady to whom he is perforce handcuffed, and who, despite his strenuous objections, insists on considering him a murderer. There is, too, one of the most amusing scenes of the year in the picture, during which the young man temporarily avoids capture by wandering into a political meeting and making an inspired campaign speech for a parliamentary candidate.

You will not, however, learn from any bare plot outline of *The 39 Steps* that every line of dialogue is civil and polished and charming; that even one brief scene, in a dour Highlander's home, has at once a romantic, religious, and melodramatic flavor in it; or that Robert Donat makes a better picaresque young man than most juvenile actors you have seen this year.

I can tell you that most of the picture was taken in the grim, gnarled Scottish Highlands; that Madeleine Carroll and Godfrey Tearle give Mr. Donat more support than he needs; that the chubby Cockney who directed it, Alfred Hitchcock, has fulfilled the promisè of a few years ago in his work, *The Man Who Knew Too Much,* and now, with *The 39 Steps,* has proved himself one of the best movie-makers in the business.

McCall's, September, 1935

THE GHOST GOES WEST

R ECENTLY, a very literate, if unsuccessful, manager of a Manhattan movie cathedral inveighed against movie critics of all types and descriptions. Pausing to sneer at the cream-puff fan reviewers for selling their dignity to Hollywood for a sheaf of movie passes, he then accused the more responsible critics of being academic and futile. Movies, he said, from the practical standpoint of a man running a 6200-seat hall, must please the masses; they must be designed to meet the understanding of the millions; therefore, they must have nothing to do with painting, music, opera, drama, or those higher art forms which demand talent, training, and a rigorous sense of selection. Those critics who attempt to seek out form, tempo, and dramatic verities in the motion picture are mumbling in the wind.

It is hardly an arresting or original thesis, this argument that movies never should be discussed as anything but "entertainment," but, granting the sound business viewpoint of the very distinguished, if amateur, movie impresario, the fact is that he neglected to describe the fundamental differences between a movie which, from a box-office standpoint, is good entertainment and one which, on the same uncritical pragmatic grounds, he considers "bad."

Actually, this old argument that popular entertainment has nothing to do with artistic ability is one of the most common manifestations of what James Truslow Adams so accurately describes as the "mucker pose." That is, no man who can write amusing stories, gay songs, or make a million people laugh really is important; the Hollywood producer, the box office manager, the sales department insist that it is an easy trick—although the producer and the theatre manager don't yet know quite how to do it.

From a critic's standpoint, *The Ghost Goes West* is a trinket. Here is a popular movie which is almost banal and certainly is dated in its satire. Based on a gentle lampoon of an American millionaire, it is a comic ghost story, during which a chain-store magnate buys a haunted Scotch castle and imports it to Florida, stone for stone, intact with its ne'er-do-well laird of the Glourie clan and the ghost of one of his unfortunate ancestors.

The ghost is made into a very real and poignant fellow, with the spirit of his father booming down at him every time he sees a pretty face. The whole picture is conceived and produced in a simple comic vein; nowhere is there any attempt to be solemn, profound, or cosmic in a manner to appeal to intellectual critics, and, from a box-office standpoint, *The Ghost Goes West* is popular, wholesome, good entertainment.

There are several reasons however, why this ghost story happens to be food for the masses.

It was written by Robert Sherwood, for one thing. Besides being

a good playwright, he is a man who invariably touches all his manuscripts with charm and a gentle grace.

It has as its leading man one of the best of the young movie
juveniles, Robert Donat, of *The 39 Steps* and *The Count of Monte
Cristo*, who plays both the unfortunate ghost, Murdock Glourie,
and his bankrupt descendant, and it has Jean Parker and Eugene
Palette lending him skilled support.

But *The Ghost Goes West* is good entertainment chiefly because it was directed by René Clair, a modest, sincere young
Frenchman who has been writing, directing, and supervising some
of the most important pictures—artistically—of the last decade.
Thus you will find beautiful photography, related music, and a
definite grace in editing and supervision which, regardless of the
childlike ghost story, make the picture refreshing, gay, and spirited.

No, there's no trick to movies. All the businessman needs to do
is to employ a fine playwright, a group of good actors, a skilled
cameraman, and put them all under the direction of a man who
understands the possibilities of the camera, and who has, besides,
a comic gift, charm, and dramatic skill—leave them to work un-
checked—and he'll get popular entertainment almost every time.

The business of unsuccessful dramatic managers blaming the
critics for their own lack of insight and judgment always riles me.
I'd intended to point out some of our mystery and supernatural
movies recently produced and to ask you to compare them with
The Ghost Goes West as a critical lesson in what movie-making is
about. On calmer thought, however, I decided that it would be
kinder to warn you and spare you the lesson.

McCall's, April, 1936

THE VOICE OF BUGLE ANN

THE MOST interesting movie of the month is the more remarkable
in that it has no right to be a picture at all. In fiction form,
"The Voice of Bugle Ann" was a long, warm-hearted story about

a Missouri farmer and his dog. Better written (by MacKinlay Kantor) than most stories of like nature, nevertheless "The Voice of Bugle Ann" hardly was substantial material for a motion picture.

Its chief asset was its verisimilitude. Kantor gave you a warm feeling of the damp nights on the Missouri ridges—his hound fanciers talking softly to one another as their dogs chased through the thickets. But the story itself was an anecdote you might carry with you out of any highland county; lucid, honest, and true enough, but a minor one if you wish to compare it with a full-bodied novel, a play, or a vigorous movie.

Tenderly related, the story told of a farmer who was devoted to his prize hound, Bugle Ann, and who killed a mean-hearted neighbor because he justifiably felt that his neighbor had done away with the dog. There were a boy and a girl in the story, but the reality and drama in the yarn were bound up in the dialogue of the farmers and in the fanatical pride and devotion which Mr. Davis had for his dog.

A good tale, but where's your movie? Your love interest? Your action? Your dramatic episodes? Your variations? Those were the questions I felt no movie director could answer, but I was almost completely wrong because The Voice of Bugle Ann in picture form remains exactly what it was on paper—the story of a man and his dog, and because of superb treatment on the part of the producer, it came out a very fine movie indeed.

The fact that the basic plot was left untouched was a small miracle in itself, but besides this achievement the producers took their little story seriously and gave to it a well-nigh foolproof cast —Lionel Barrymore and Dudley Digges in themselves almost constitute a cast, but this time they hardly could have been chosen more accurately, with Mr. Barrymore as the simple dog fancier and Mr. Digges as a sour, warped, hard-talking farmer. Charles Grapewin, Maureen O'Sullivan, and Spring Byington bring up an assured support.

Of course, with such fragile material even a simple story and a fine cast might have spelled nothing very much had not the director caught the feeling of the country and the people—he even manages to record a foxhound's baying that sounds distinctive and dramatic, and you really can't ask for much more in the way of production.

The whole picture could stand some pruning, and we might have been spared Senator Vest's famous eulogy delivered in a Missouri courtroom many years ago, but Mr. Barrymore makes it sound as though he had just thought of it and if, as is very likely, you never had to recite it in grade school, you probably won't find it as hard to take as a veteran dog eulogizer.

McCall's, May, 1936

MODERN TIMES

ONE OF the most important pictures of the year and a very amusing trinket have a common virtue in that the photography in both of them dates back to the pre-Sennett, or tin-type, era of pictures.

There has been a great deal of loose talk in recent years about the art of photography, but you won't find any pictorial virtuosity in Chaplin's *Modern Times*. The factory set is very fine and the street scenes are clear and lucid, but you'll find no symbolical lights and shadows, no polished shading in the camera work—and for a very good reason: the camera is the least important prop in a Chaplin production.

I might take off from this little essay on the art of the camera to advise you that *Modern Times* is the best picture Chaplin has made and that, for all its old-fashioned silent devices, its unnecessary captions, and awkward story tricks, it has dignity, feeling, and power. It is a comedy of poverty, the comedy Chaplin always has played. But this time it is not a never-never land of a circus, or any back lot, or any waterfront. It is a poverty of our times, and it is very real.

It is also, of course, very funny. The master pantomimist has not lost his touch; in fact, he has become at last a funny man who feels deeply the horror of poverty—the sort of funny man he has for years wanted to be and has, in *Modern Times,* finally created.

His camera work is as simple as a child's drawing—out of disdain, true, rather than design—but some of the light-and-shadow and cockeyed angle boys might take note that your meaning and direction are a great deal more important in movies than your tools.

McCall's, May, 1936

THE PLOW THAT BROKE THE PLAINS

Allowed by an indulgent editor to discuss a picture I myself wrote, I find it an embarrassing assignment. The production is a three-reel documentary musical picture called *The Plow That Broke The Plains.* The story: a brief history of the Great Plains from the time of the first cattle ranches to the present day.

We had two prime objectives in making the picture: one, to show audiences a specific and exciting section of the country; the other, to portray the events which led up to one of the major catastrophies in American history—to show, in other words, the Great Drought which is now going into its sixth year.

Two very distinguished workmen, Ralph Steiner and Paul Strand, took some of the most beautiful pictures ever made for any production, and in doing so justified a plea critics have made to Hollywood for a decade—namely, "Take your cameras into the country and show us what it looks like."

The composer, Virgil Thomson, wrote what I think is the best musical score ever composed for an American movie—not only because he is a good musician but because, understanding the story, he worked for months making his music an integral part of the production.

Thus, with some outstanding photography and music, *The Plow That Broke The Plains* is an unusual motion picture which might have been a really great one had the story and the construction been up to the rest of the workmanship. As it is, it tells the story of the Plains, and it tells it with some emotional value—an emotion that springs out of the soil itself. Our heroine is the grass, our villain the sun and the wind, our players the actual farmers living in the Plains country. It is a melodrama of nature—the tragedy of turning grass into dust, a melodrama that only Carl Sandburg or Willa Cather, perhaps, could tell as it should be told.

You will not see the full horror of the dust storms in the picture, a horror that drove men to kill their cattle because they could not stand their ceaseless bellowing, the horror of children choking and dying of dust pneumonia. You will not see it because we had limited funds and a skeleton staff, but you will see enough of the Plains and the Great Drought to make it worth your while.

McCall's, July, 1936

WINTERSET; REMBRANDT

IT IS not uncommon to find moments of beauty, humor or even greatness during a month's movie-going, but this has been an unusual month in that not one but two very fine productions were released—unusual because for once not photography, acting, direction nor technical proficiency but words made them unusual, and mighty brave words they are, too.

The better of the two in every way is *Winterset*, the screen translation of Maxwell Anderson's lyric melodrama. You may feel as I did when I heard similar words describing this play—an uneasy feeling that poetry hardly goes with gangsters, or that, having wanted to write beautiful words, Mr. Anderson feared to choose austere, heroic subjects for them and attempted to create popular characters in order to insure popular success, and then clothed them in fine garments.

Actually, however, *Winterset* does not deal with crime and poverty, nor with man's inhumanity to man in general: it is a bitter, mocking paean to Justice—and not the blindfolded Greek statue, but the sense of justice that led the State of Massachusetts to imprison Sacco and Vanzetti in 1920, to hold them there for many long years, to call on a special committee, including the president of Harvard University, to review the evidence and then, in the face of world-wide protest, to electrocute them. This is neither the time nor the place to discuss the Sacco-Vanzetti case, even if I were versed enough in the story to deal with it, but it is foolish to attempt to explain *Winterset* to you without establishing the fact that it is a play about a specific criminal trial and without informing you further that the great playwright who wrote the picture dealt with the same trial once before, in even more powerful and, at times, more lyrical words, in an unsuccessful play called "Gods of the Lightning."

And now for the picture. As is true of all adaptations, you will not get an exact re-creation of the play on the screen. Sometimes the close-ups bring out the words more forcefully, sometimes (including the horrific scene during which a presumably murdered man suddenly appears, smeared with gore, in the doorway to face his murderer) the close-ups detract from the power of the story because you are able to feel and see only one character at that precise, blood-curdling moment.

Then, too, the very last note of the symphony, the last sighing chorus, suddenly changes key in the picture. In a mocking, bitter drama of frustration, it was logical and necessary that, having found his Holy Grail, the hero should die ignominiously. In the picture, the music suddenly changes into a gentle waltz, and the hero and his girl walk hand-in-hand into a new world—a dramatic, practical, and psychological impossibility. But if you never saw the play, or if it never stirred you to any deep reflection, you will not mind the happy screen ending because, having felt called upon to correct a great manuscript, the producers, it is only fair to admit, did it shrewdly and painlessly.

The story, as I have tried to imply, is not a story in the usual stage or movie sense. It is not a tale of situations or incidents but a tone poem in which murder, starvation or love are not introduced to you in the usual polite dramatic form, "Meet Mr. So-and-so, he is the hero." On the contrary, the hero cocks his head to the sky and speaks from his heart and not from the conventional dialogue of everyday life, and his speeches lift you from all consciousness of ordinary theatre-going into a high feeling of elation at hearing fine words spoken beautifully.

With one or two exceptions, the players are for once up to their work. Margo, as the strange waif dancing awkwardly to the strains of a barrel organ under the cobwebs of Brooklyn Bridge; Edward Ellis, as the judge who wanders the earth because he too fears he sent an innocent man to his death; Paul Guilfoyle, as the fiddle-playing Judas who dares not confess the truth about the murder; and finally young Burgess Meredith, who gives a truly great performance—not even Mr. Anderson could find fault with them.

The other picture in which you can hear words not usual to the movie sound machines is Alexander Korda's production, *Rembrandt*, which has neither the form, depth nor beauty of *Winterset* because it is a portrait, a series of historical episodes, rather than a play; but it is amusing and pretty to see. It also is very stirring to hear because, for the first time I can remember, someone has thought to bring some of the language of the King James Bible to the screen.

Most of you, of course, will go to see it because of Charles Laughton in his characterization of the great Dutchman, and I will go along with you and concede him one of the best character actors of our time.

Mr. Korda, as usual, spares nothing in his production—the winter scenes in Holland would be refreshing if half as well done simply because no one in Hollywood ever heard of Holland and wouldn't show it on a screen even if they had. But there is more than photography and setting in the production: Gertrude Lawrence, as the bitter, shrewish, rich wife, and Elsa Lanchester (Mrs. Laughton), as the gentle country wife, are very happily cast.

McCall's, February, 1937

AFTER THE THIN MAN

I CANNOT think of an exact word to describe it, but occasionally in the theatre you find a play which, besides being popular and .successful, arouses a loyalty and sympathy from audience and critics alike—a play which may even be full of dramatic weaknesses, but which you embrace as completely and understanding as that first sweetheart, who, although bowlegged and slightly popeyed, seemed all the more attractive for having such peculiarities.

As few people ever write or make pictures with any deep regard for their work, it is even rarer to find a warm, gay, and charming movie than it is to discover plays of that nature; there is so much money, so much exaggerated excitement, so many little heroes connected with motion picture production, that it is more often by accident than by design that you run across a spontaneous bit of writing or acting in a movie.

The Thin Man was such an exception—and the producers were taking a chance when they attempted to make a sequel and to endow it with the same insouciant air that made the original such a delight.

Thus I am happy to report that, while it will not be as fresh to you as the original Dashiell Hammett production, *After The Thin Man* is a very successful sequel.

The picture opens very slowly, and more or less seeks to introduce again the idyllic married life of Mr. and Mrs. Nick Charles and their wirehair, Asta. As a matter of fact, for the first ten or fifteen minutes I was a bit frightened for fear the whole story would turn into a dog picture. However, the sets, the photography and the staging in these first few scenes are superb, if overdone. Then one of Mr. Hammett's charming characters, a blackmailing ne'er-do-well, is murdered, and Mr. Powell and Miss Loy are off to the races again.

As is true of practically everything Mr. Hammett writes, the plot is perfectly cockeyed, but it doesn't make any difference because his characters are so brilliantly and gaily drawn.

Joseph Calleia as a night-club proprietor, James Stewart as a rich young San Franciscan, Dorothy McNulty (a newcomer) as a healthy night club singer, and Sam Levine as a patient, weary police officer, all help Mr. Powell track his way softly through the inextricable maze of the story in a most satisfactory manner. Miss Loy, as I have pointed out before, seems to grow more charming with each production—the remark still holds.

Elissa Landi tried too hard to be a jittery young neurotic and Jessie Ralph (as is true of almost all older character women in the movies) seemed to be trying to blow the cameras clear out of the studio—the introductory night-club number should have been cut down—but enough, enough. Mr. Hammett and his associates did it again and added a gay sequel to the memory of the most charming picture of last season. I refuse to chide them further for minor errors.

McCall's, March, 1937

FIRE OVER ENGLAND

THE PAST month has been as exciting a one as I can remember in this business—because all the pictures I have seen have been unusual either in design or in subject matter. In fact, to do a thorough, academic job, I should begin this report with an essay on religious intolerance, starting with the foundation of Protestant England and the collapse of the Holy Roman Empire, going from there to the early days of Puritan New England, and ending with a discussion of modern religious belief. Specifically, *Fire Over England* is a costume picture dealing with Elizabeth and Philip II; *Maid of Salem* is a story of the witch burnings in New England; *Green Light* is a drama of modern religion.

Of the three, *Fire Over England* is far and away the best movie. It has a better story, it is played superbly, and it has great beauty. Known to the trade as an "English" picture, it was made in London but produced by a Hungarian, Alexander Korda; supervised by a German, Erich Pommer; directed by an American, William

K. Howard; and photographed by a Chinese, James Wong Howe.

Even these highly talented internationalists were afraid of censors, because they did not follow completely the first-rate story originally written by A. E. W. Mason. As he told it, an English sailor and his son are captured by a Spanish nobleman; the father is turned over to the Inquisition to be burned and tortured; the son is turned loose by the Spaniard because the old men once were friends. The boy becomes a spy for Elizabeth and manages to get clear to Philip himself before he is detected; he makes his escape and is knighted by Elizabeth for his heroism in the destruction of the Spanish Armada.

All this you will see in *Fire Over England*. You will, however, at the end of the picture, have to listen to some very tiresome stump speeches about old England, and you will not see the awful meeting of the old boy and what the Inquisition left of his father—an episode which in the novel gave meaning and substance to the character of the hero, and which made the war a very real story of religious intolerance—an episode which would have made *Fire Over England* really a fiery drama.

However, right up until the Empire conclusion substituted in the picture, Mr. Howard created as fine a movie as I ever have seen, and he cast it with almost an uncanny judgment. Leslie Banks as Leicester, Raymond Massey as Philip II, and Laurence Olivier as the youngster, give their characters not only great dignity but sharp and lucid outlines; even they, however, are overshadowed by Flora Robson. Miss Robson's Queen Elizabeth is a masterpiece—ungainly, ugly, capricious, old and tired, yet dynamic, regal, and appealing; it is a perfect bit of character playing.

Fire Over England is one of those rare things: a fine job of collaboration on the part of actors, writers, costumers, musicians, technicians and producers, but Director Howard deserves most of the credit for the picture. His cool, sweeping Spanish sets, his quiet love scenes, his feeling of imminent desperate action, his delightful ballads—there are a hundred intimate details in the production proving him what he long has been in his quiet way: one of the finest movie makers in Hollywood.

McCall's, April, 1937

Peroration No. 3

WHEN MOVIE-GOERS HAVE ENOUGH

THE ONLY time I ever had the privilege of meeting Will Hays privately, he opened the interview by leaning across his desk, smiling from ear to ear (a disconcerting feat in itself), and remarking, "Everyone in America has two businesses—his own and the movies."

While I for one would be the last person in the world to question Mr. Hays, either on a point of honesty or profundity, I do think he has neglected his duty to his employers, because I'm sure he never has told them this theory. But if the movies belong to all of us, I should like, as a minor stockholder, to bring in my annual report to the management and tell them how to run their—pardon, I mean *our*—business. And by running, I mean managing—writing, editing, directing and casting have nothing to do with the business of the industry.

Item Number One: *No more double bills*. I feel we all are agreed on this point. Either a movie is worth seeing or it isn't, but it certainly isn't worth it if, after you have sat through the trailers, next week's announcements and the newsreel, instead of presenting what you paid your money to see, they first show you a *Turn Off The Moon* or *Outcasts of Poker Flat*. Even if you do like the feature you came to see, you are half-asleep, half-blind and hungry by the time it comes on.

Item Number Two: *Better short subjects*. This, of course, takes care of item one, and if you say, "Well, I've been saying that for years," you are quite right. We've all been saying it for years—that is my point. It's high time this word got to the management.

I can tell you a few things which have prevented development of better short subjects. One of them is the fact that no one can get rich overnight making short pictures. You can make a profit—oh, yes—say two or three hundred percent profit. But Hollywood producers, accustomed as they are to having to carry cash in their pockets, never in the history of the industry have planned beyond the immediate picture they are producing.

They expect that one to pay for all their past mistakes, and to make enough money to keep them in yachts. They never have produced movies on the theory that made many a company prosperous, which is: "You never go broke making a small profit."

Yet, despite the fact that no major studio ever has seriously considered entertaining its own customers by seeing to the thirty-minute pictures—which are just as valuable to the audience as the hundred-minute shows—two or three people have proved that the short picture can be amusing and important, and can make millions of friends.

Walt Disney, with his *Mickey Mouse* and his *Silly Symphony*, is worth more to audiences than just about eighty percent of the producers in the business.

The March of Time, while it presents news instead of movies, nevertheless presents that news better than the corporations who own newsreel outfits—it has several million friends and has proved itself a profitable venture.

Laurel and Hardy will bring people into a theatre, whereas a triple bill composed of *John Mead's Woman*, *The Woman I Love* and *Love on the Run*, all presented with a turkey and a set of china as a premium for the housewives thrown in, will make the theatre owner happy if he draws the high school baseball team and two traveling salesmen past his ticket window.

Why doesn't someone besides the big studios make short pictures? For the reason that it is very, very difficult for anyone besides the eight corporations to make movies in America. Thus the answer to this item is: first-rate short pictures do away with double bills—first-rate short subjects are profitable—they are not profitable enough, however, to interest the big boys—they won't let anyone else make pictures.

Item Number Three: *It isn't any fun to go to a movie theatre.* The excitement of that moment when the house lights are lowered, the orchestra is silent, the audience settles down, and the curtain goes up is one of the most glamorous and thrilling moments of the theatre.

That is, it should be. In 1928–1929 the movie industry was whirled aloft by Wall Street and, among other things, the industry built hundreds of atrocious, ghastly mockeries of architecture, dripping with gilt filigree, illuminated by undertakers' lights, gaping with railroad terminal corridors, and called them theatres.

During the Depression, the carpets wore through, the gilt tarnished, and the corridors became dank, but with recovery they fixed that. They installed loudspeakers in the lobbies, banners and candy shops and phonograph stands in the corridors, so that now when you go to the movies you have the feeling you have wandered into the poorest section of Coney Island instead of a theatre.

Inside the theatre you find more serious, if less visible, faults. The sound equipment in many theatres has not been overhauled for years, and where I may honestly recommend, say, *Maytime*, to you as a vigorous, modern musical picture with charming melodies and great rousing choruses, by the time it reaches your theatre the melodies may sound like an echo from the radio shop down the street, and the choruses like a sawmill on a busy day.

We don't go to the theatre because we have to—it should be fun. And all we need is a comfortable seat, peace and quiet, and a good show to feel we have our money's worth—not a basket of china, a bingo game, a chocolate bar, and an announcement about *next* week's picture. Which brings us to item four.

Item Number Four: *The trailer must go.* Even when the producers do make a good picture, they handicap themselves by rushing out a wild-eyed, noisy, meaningless short picture in which we are informed that the most gigantic, colossal, and overpowering production since *Ben Hur* will play in the theatre next week.

There are three reasons why such advertising is silly. One is that we are in the theatre, and we heard *last* week that the picture we are presently to see was colossal; we know better by the time the evening is over, so why should we be interested in next week's picture? Secondly, it may be that the advertised production is amusing or gay, but the trailer is just as likely to sour you in advance as it is to sell you on the merits of the production, simply because the trailer itself is a hodge-podge of meaningless scenes, whereas the picture it advertises may have been made with intelligence and skill.

And, lastly, the trailer takes up time. The power and the handicap of the screen as a dramatic medium is that it is never static—something must move on the screen, and the time spent showing two or three trailers is not only a bore, but it irritates and annoys the audience to a point where it is not in any mood to enjoy a show.

Item Number Five: *The critics.* For years every newspaper in the country has abased itself and allowed Hollywood to review its own pictures. There are not more than a dozen newspapers in the country that believe the faith of their readers is more important than the advertising revenue from motion picture theatres. Thus, few of you can depend upon your daily newspaper for any sort of honest comment about the movies playing in your town. Week in and week out they are all advertised and announced with a whoop-de-do that is as monotonous as it is misleading. The result is that audiences pay to see good pictures and stay away from the lemons despite the newspapers.

I presume it is too much to expect from the studio savants, but I do feel that they would prosper if they themselves demanded a better class of movie reviewers from the publishers, instead of the office boys, fourth assistant society editors, and relatives now assigned on most daily papers to do movie reviewing. One result would be that audiences would trust the *good* notices for a change, and, as even double bills and raffles won't get them in to see poor pictures, the industry, as well as the press, might gain.

These are a few of the things I believe all 70,000,000 of us who go to movies every week agree upon.

Fortunately, movie-going is a habit and not a necessity, so any time the stockholders, all 70,000,000 of us, get bored enough to stay away from the double bills and the gingerbread Coney Island palaces and the bingo games, the management will know that the handwriting, if not on the wall, is on the books.

McCall's, August, 1937

ZOLA; THEY WON'T FORGET

A BOUT a week before this report was due, I had decided that the most important news of the month was the announcement from Will Hays that Hollywood was going to enter the educational field in a large way. Later, however, in looking over these columns for the last two months, I discovered I had indulged in quite a bit of social and political *obiter dicta*, and while I enjoy being the village Communist, I felt, "Well, Mr. Hays will always be there, and this month you'd best just report on movies, who's in them, and how well they were made, if only for the sake of variety."

But by the time the week was out, Hollywood released four pictures which deal with social or political history, and two of them are based on two of the most brutal chapters ever written in the black book of race hatred, so I'm forced to the soap box again.

All the best productions of the month were based on history of a sort: *Zola*, the Dreyfus case; *They Won't Forget*, the Leo Frank murder trial; *The Toast of New York*, the days of Jim Fiske and Daniel Drew; and, while it is a musical comedy, even *High, Wide and Handsome* sings a story of the discovery of oil in western Pennsylvania.

Probably the most unusual and courageous of the four is *Zola*—not because it is as savage, uncompromising, and direct as *They Won't Forget*, but because it deals with an international scandal that has not yet cleared off the battleground of French politics. Few of you remember the Leo Frank case; few of you lack some sort of vague recollection of Captain Dreyfus, his exile to Devil's Island, and his defense by Emile Zola.

The recorded facts of the Dreyfus case are: one Alfred Dreyfus, of Jewish descent, a brilliant officer and a member of the general staff of the French Army, was arrested in 1894 on a charge of selling military secrets to the Germans.

Due to the efforts of Zola and a young editor named Clemenceau, Captain Dreyfus was re-tried in 1899, again found guilty, but this time with "extenuating circumstances" which led to a pardon;

not until 1906 was Captain Dreyfus declared innocent and the victim of a forgery, at which time his military honors were restored and he was made a Major in the army. Even then, the brutal, anti-Semitic wave still was flowing so bitterly in Paris that the martyred Major was shot and killed two years later by one Gregori at the time when Zola's remains were moved to the Pantheon.

The picture itself is divided almost deliberately into two acts: in the first, you have a portrait study of Emile Zola by Paul Muni —a study which, superb as it is, necessarily is rather slow and unimportant.

The second act is built around Zola's trial for criminal libel, brought because of his book, "J'Accuse," which hammered at practically everyone in France except Stavisky, who wasn't around then, and which forced a reopening of the dismal Dreyfus case. Here you have almost an hour of motion picture taking place in a courtroom; you have a motion picture dealing with justice and not unrequited love, marriage or divorce—an hour during which you have little going on except oration, yet it is as emotional and stirring an hour as you'll ever spend in a movie theatre. Of course, the sheer theme of justice triumphant would not of itself have been so exciting had it not been handled so well by the director and by Mr. Muni.

There is no love story and no comic interest in *Zola*. It's a grave story told with great dignity and superbly played and produced.

From the time you hear the band play "Dixie" until Claude Rains looks out the window as he says, "I wonder," *They Won't Forget* is as nerve-wracking a picture as you've ever seen, or will see for many a day. Not adapted, but built completely on Ward Greene's terse and bitter novel, "Death in the Deep South," Mervyn LeRoy's production is not only an honest picture, but an example of real movie-making.

He had a straightforward story to start with—he didn't change one scene. He had a terrific melodrama; with the exception of Claude Rains, he didn't try to tell his story with well-known or type-cast movie actors. I've never seen but three people before out of the entire cast, yet because of the story and the direction, all the unknowns—Lana Turner as the young girl who is found down the elevator shaft, Trevor Bardette as her poor-white brother, Clinton Rosemond, the Negro janitor, the reporters, the Confederate soldiers—all of them seem to be polished and experienced actors.

Alan Josling as the reporter, and Claude Rains as an ambitious small-town Southern attorney, deserve some credit in their own right, as they give by their characterizations even more power than LeRoy could have poured into the production without them.

They Won't Forget has almost everything you could ask for in a melodrama. It is a mystery story; it is a story of a great present-day murder trial, with radio, special correspondents and spectators and all the stage setting we get with modern jurisprudence; it is a story—still at this writing being retold in Decatur, Alabama—of the deep-seated ancient social antipathy between the small-town Southerner and the urban Northerner; and it is, underneath all, the story of a school teacher who dies because of the ambitions of a reporter and an attorney.

The Warner Brothers bang out some rather curious movies during a season, but I think it is only fair to mention the fact that the Brothers produced both *Zola* and *They Won't Forget*, which puts them at the head of the class right now.

McCall's, October, 1937

SNOW WHITE

IF I WERE asked to list the most important movie activity of 1937 ten years from now, I should have only one item to report: Walt Disney made a full-length movie. And this one event may save the industry as it is now organized.

Ordinarily, I would not write an article about Walt Disney because I feel when an artist is accepted and beloved by millions of people all over the world, it is fairly gratuitous on the part of a critic to "discover" him. But the fact that Disney has made a full-length musical color picture from Grimm's fairy tale, "Snow White and the Seven Dwarfs," has rather important implications.

Snow White is not important just because it is a longer and more elaborate Disney. It is important, for one thing, because the colors themselves are beautiful as well as utilitarian; you see not only a series of lovely panels, but a continuity of color effects ranging from bright effects to sombre and terrifying shades, all in perfect harmony with the mood of the characters and with the musical score—a flowing use of color that will be the despair of directors working with human actors for many years to come.

And *Snow White* is not a childish little production for the children; it has a mature and pathetic note that far surpasses any emotional feeling Disney hitherto has created with his little figures. There is enough of the hate and sorrow of the old Black Forest tale in it so that it is indeed dramatic at times, even though for the most part it has simply Disney violence, than which there is no greater violence ever created on stage or screen.

But perhaps I can better convey to you some of the importance of this animated feature by briefly explaining the material with which the picture was made (and I do not intend to go into an exhaustive report on how many men drew how many pictures during the two years it was in production).

What you will see is a series of drawings in color, charmingly and skillfully drawn. You will hear voices that uncannily fit the drawn characters; you will hear chirps, and snorts, and grunts that truly fit the animals, who also have characters that remain in key throughout the tale.

You will hear a musical score longer than any you've ever heard in any picture, and, for my money, better than any musical score you've ever heard with any picture.

And, most important, you will find that the drawings, the colors, the narration, the sound effects, and the music all have been put together with consummate skill and intensity so that overall you have what is most important: the very mood and charm and fey emotion of a fairy tale. You have, in short, the one artist in Hollywood turning out his masterpiece.

And when I say the one artist, I do not mean to use the word loosely, nor do I mean to dismiss lightly a great many talented and sincere men who are employed by the movies.

But Disney is as unique today as Chaplin was when he produced *Shoulder Arms, The Kid, The Gold Rush*, and his other great pictures. Like Chaplin, he is his own author, director, and actor; like Chaplin he lives, eats, and sleeps his work, and there is no board of directors to tell him how to make pictures, nor what the public wants, nor what stars to use.

He is completely divorced from Hollywood in fact as well as fancy. His studio is miles out in the wilds somewhere; his workmen grind away in a modern industrial plant; his equipment is unique and designed solely for him. And while I have heard many sour rumors about his policies as an employer, I have not bothered about them because I do not feel they are important. Animation itself is a back-breaking job, and Disney is not satisfied with anything less than perfection.

And the tortuous business of fitting color to every drawing, of timing the drawings, of scoring sound effects and music and of rescoring them, and of changing endless scenes would drive anyone crazy save a man who lives only for his work.

But when I said Disney was the one artist in Hollywood I did not mean to imply he deserved such stature because he was clever or hard-working or successful. Actually, he is the only man in the entire business who brings his own individuality to his work—the only man who says exactly what he wants without any compromise whatsoever. And there is not a writer, a director, a musician, not an actor making movies in the country today who can claim half that independence.

Thus it is not strange that with *Snow White* Disney is breaking every known taboo set up during the years by the producers. First, he is taking a short "filler" subject and making it into a million-and-a-half-dollar feature. Secondly, he has produced a fairy tale, and, finally, he did it without any conferences, any advice, and with his own money. There is no question that *Snow White* will be successful. Disney already is launched on a second production, *Bambi*, the Felix Salten tale of a deer, but the subject matter, while admirably suited to animation, is relatively unimportant.

What is important is that we have at least one man who is making movies because he loves to do it, and who is not worrying about best-sellers, radio (he won't sell Mickey over the air), censors (can you imagine a Disney production of "It Can't Happen Here"?), Will Hays, or supervisors. And, finally, he is helping to save a business by making movies that win friends for the screen itself—that make it fun to go to the theatre.

McCall's, February, 1938

A YANK AT OXFORD

THE BIGGEST mistake anyone could make about Hollywood is in expecting to meet someone in Hollywood who is interested in motion pictures. Mind you, there is no other topic of conversation here than pictures; but in Hollywood that word has nothing to do with celluloid, or sound, or cameras. On the contrary, all conversation is carried on in a strong jargon which has to do with "Schenck, Zanuck, Goldwyn, Warner, Spitz" etc., and which strikes the ear for the first few days as being one of the lesser-known Arabic dialects.

It is a gracious town and, in many ways, a generous one. But one thing you cannot do: you cannot talk about dramatic construction, music, photography, or anything having to do with the methods of motion-picture production; that is a low-caste interest shared only by cameramen, sound engineers, and the cutters and other hired hands who merely put movies together.

I was fortunate enough to attend a preview of Robert Taylor's new picture, *A Yank at Oxford*, with some very distinguished Hollywood celebrities. We slipped out to the outskirts of town because the producer wanted to get a spontaneous reaction from a regular movie audience, and except for a small advertisement in two or three newspapers, the showing was presented in great secrecy. The picture was produced in England, presumably because of the fact that Oxford is in England. As it happened, the British would not allow the company to work in the ancient halls of Oxford, but it was convenient for them to have the university close at hand so they could at least run up and look at it once in a while.

The story concerns the athletic star of a small Midwestern college who is given a scholarship to Oxford and who on the very train up to the university alienates the British by his braggadocio. To make it worse, the loud-mouthed Midwesterner is as good as he claims to be, and he wins a freshman track tryout by running in his cap and gown. The American is promptly "de-bagged" (pants off to us) by his classmates, in the most effective scene in the picture, and forthwith decides to go home, but he hears the chimes in Magdalen tower and his scout persuades him to stick it out.

At this point we might have expected to have seen something of Oxford and its customs, but there is a girl who runs in and out of the quarters as though it were Taylor's own *alma mater*, Pomona, and not the most bachelor university in the world, and a college widow, with whom practically the entire student body spends most of its time. There is no time for even one scholastic sequence.

I presume with some thought you might puzzle out the conclusion of the picture yourself: Mr. Taylor strokes the crew to victory and gallantly takes the blame for his enemy's escapade, and becomes the most popular fellow ever to attend Oxford.

Two of the English players, Vivien Leigh, as the college widow, and Edmund Gwenn, as a testy don, give superb performances, but Mr. Taylor, being Mr. Taylor, is content to be himself.

I mentioned the fact that I went to a preview simply because it was interesting to me to listen to the inside comments. First, I was told the picture would make tons of money because, for one thing, there were a hundred high-school boys and girls waiting outside the theatre for Mr. Taylor's autograph, proof enough, it seemed, that Mr. Taylor was the idol of the youth of the country.

Again, I was told that *Brown of Harvard*, made some years ago by the same company, was a successful picture, and as *Yank at Oxford* had the same plot, why shouldn't it be a wow? Not to mention the fact that *Navy Blue and Gold* has the same story, and it is successful. And to my murmurings that Mr. Taylor seemed churlish and a bit of a cad, and that the love scenes were poorly written, and that you couldn't tell what time of day, or what month, or what year the picture was being played in, I was told, "But it will make a fortune." I leave the proof in your hands.

McCall's, April, 1938

THE ADVENTURES OF CHICO

WHILE it has no love story, and only two actors, and no expensive scenery, *The Adventures of Chico* is probably the best of the adventure stories of the month. Written, directed, and photographed by two cameramen, the Woodard brothers, it is the story of a Mexican boy and his father, and of their life in the jungles of Mexico.

It is such a simple movie that it gathers a tremendous emotional power—a power developing from the fact that from the very first scene in the picture you feel you are living under the blazing Mexican sky. The Mexican child is so ingratiating that you forget immediately you are watching a movie and feel as though you were a spectator, a visitor in Mexico, watching the quiet and unaffected happenings of a peon family.

While Chico is the star of the picture, his adventures are with the goats, the birds, the deer, the panthers, and the snakes of his jungle.

There is a suggestion of a plot in the movie: the boy befriends a chaparral bird, and the bird in turn saves his life by killing a rattlesnake that slides upon him while he is taking his siesta in the shade of his hut.

But it is the rare and consistent beauty, the suspended, as it were, action of the picture, that is important—a consistency you never find in ordinary movies simply because there are not many Woodard brothers in the movies. These two young men for years have been photographing nature pictures and distributing them under the title of *The Struggle To Live*.

Having worked with animals for years, they found their Mexican boy (where, they won't say, for fear Hollywood will find him and make a star of him—which they feel, oddly enough, would ruin his life), took him and an old peon into the jungles, and for one year worked to reproduce on film a feeling of the simplicity of the Mexican, the heat of his jungle, and the animal life around him.

They gambled with their own money and talent and produced a rare type of American picture—rare because so few men in Hollywood ever break away from the standardized commercial story and attempt an original motion picture. *Chico* is really an adventure because it is new, honest, and simple and beautiful to watch.

McCall's, May, 1938

MEN MAKE STEEL

THE MOST exciting picture I have seen in many weeks is neither a short nor a feature; there are no stars, and there is no plot or romance in the production. It was produced for the U.S. Steel Corporation by Roland Reed and photographed in Technicolor, and is called, none too aptly, *Men Make Steel.*

This four-reel color movie, on strict grounds of dialogue, editing, and music, is not a first-class piece of work. You have to listen to Edwin C. Hill's roaring voice, the musical score is weak and inept, and the film editor jumps from one location to another, leaving you a bit confused.

But it is paradoxical that this industrial educational movie should turn out to be the most beautiful color picture ever made, and for the color alone, I recommend *Men Make Steel* to you. The dull blues of the gigantic furnaces, the red and gold fountains of molten steel, the squat Bessemers pouring their great ladles against a dark sky—these are thrilling and awe-inspiring photographs.

And the men themselves are fairly impressive; bemused and deliberate, and surprisingly young, the steel workers bring a dignity to their work that is typical of all tough working men, but that lends a conviction to the picture no routine cast of film players could achieve. Of course, the real novelty of the picture is its subject matter. In a country built of steel, living in an economy that is governed by steel, few of you have an idea of the labor, the skill, or the gigantic equipment that is incorporated in the structure of Big Steel.

Here is a picture that will explain many headlines to you—headlines about Aliquippa and the Mahoning Valley, and Pittsburgh, Steubenville, Wheeling, and Weirton.

It is an advertising picture, or, if you will, a propaganda movie. But you can take from the movie exactly what you bring to it: you can marvel at the intelligence that went into the conception of such an industry; you can wonder how men can work so placidly with red-hot metal; you can wonder why so many of the men are under forty and worry about old-age employment—you can, in short, build a left wing, a center, or a right-wing philosophy from the picture.

Except for the banal close-up of a fellow tucking a paycheck in his pocket, and except for one final bellow from Edwin C. Hill about the importance of the industry, there is no statement of any kind in the picture about economics or politics—the picture is about steel, and it shows you steel being made.

As far as Hollywood is concerned, the producers will say, "It's an advertising picture and has no box office worth," and let it go at that—that is, they will say that if they continue the policy they have maintained for years in the movie industry. But whatever they say, within the year these so-called industrial pictures are going to have significant effect on the entire movie world. There is visible proof that by their own limitations Hollywood producers have lost millions of potential customers.

For the past ten years we have been thinking a great deal about the facts of this country—of its land, its social and economic problems, and about its great factories. Yet in the last decade no movie company has even attempted to use the actual drama of our national life as photographic material. To be sure, we did have the gangster cycle, but when you saw *Underworld* you saw them all. And there have been a few faint-hearted attempts at using industrial locations inside regular movie romantic plots: we had *Black*

Legion and, probably the best of the lot (which bred a flock of imitations), *Come And Get It*. But think of the swing bands, the crooners, and the vaudeville acts we get in our short subjects! Think of the newsreel, that neither time, fact nor fancy can change!

It is in this field that—Edwin C. Hill and the confused editing notwithstanding—*Men Make Steel* has no competition as far as I'm concerned.

If a movie company spent several hundred thousand dollars making four-reel pictures, there is no question they would eventually go bankrupt, and I can accept the argument from a producer that U.S. Steel can afford to spend more money making a short picture about the steel business than any company that has to live by selling movies to theatres.

On the other hand, if Hollywood demands the right—or at least has the power, at present—to make all the pictures we see on all the screens in the country; if it consistently refuses, through ignorance of the country around it, to experiment with new subject material, and new methods of using it, then, no matter who produces the picture, some organization, or group of organizations, will inevitably produce better and more imaginative movies.

And that is why I stated earlier that within the year the so-called industrial film should have a profound influence on the motion-picture business.

Many corporations for years have been producing short pictures —for their salesmen, for educational groups, and for home projectors. Next year, however, there are two World's Fairs (you couldn't expect us to be content with just one World's Fair) and there will be probably over a hundred movies made by business firms and industrial organizations, and there will be government movies to show along with their exhibits.

Offhand, that sounds like a rather dull business, but consider this: the corporations, unlike some Hollywood producers, have learned quite a bit about movie-making during the past ten years, and they will probably spend a great deal of money on their movies.

But the real value of these pictures is that they will show millions of people for the first time just how many bewildering machines, processes, and gadgets make up an industrial civilization.

Thus, as has happened before, it may be that a group of non-theatrical corporations may come to the rescue, and make the factual film exciting enough to give audiences once again a curiosity about movies.

The great German directors rescued Hollywood in the twenties with their new technique and their new material, and after them the Russians gave the technicians some new ideas. It would not be too farfetched to predict that U.S. Steel has offered them still a new, and as yet unexplored, photographic world in which to work; that is, the world in which we happen to be living.

McCall's, July, 1938

THE GRAND ILLUSION

THE FRENCH picture, *The Grand Illusion*, is a war story without any war in it, and one so simply, and at times crudely, told that you might think it had been produced way back in the old silent movie days.

The very fact that it has no great airplane battles, that it has no huge so-called production sequences, only adds to the great power and tragedy you will find in this picture. (It has English titles, but you don't need them because the story is so simply told even a child can understand it.)

Mr. Renoir's movie concerns a group of French officers who are interned in a German prison camp—two camps, to be exact. As Captain de Boildieu remarks, as a tennis court is meant for tennis, a polo field for polo, then a prison camp is something you escape from. But *The Grand Illusion* is not a melodrama of escape; it is, by the grace of four great actors, a study of characters—a study of men in war.

There are so many delicate shadings of character in the picture I hesitate to attempt any description of the various ways in which Renoir paints their portraits for you with his camera. One thing I know you will see and understand: the simple way in which Renoir tells his story. And that is movie-making. You will see no white-hot sets, with every detail apparent to the eye in a second. You will find no great emotional, "Oh, the pity of it all!" scenes. You will see Captain de Boildieu, the gentleman officer; Marechal, the mechanic who became a pilot; his friend Rosenthal, politely trying to escape from the tragic hospitality of the Prussian, Von Rauffenstein.

Every moment, every gesture of these men becomes highly important to you. You feel, before you leave them, that you know their table manners, their small talk, their most intimate secrets. And you feel, finally, when you see Marechal and his friend Rosenthal staggering far in the distance across a snow-covered Alpine pass, a most profound compassion—and despair—for them.

There are some crude scenes, and there is some awkward editing in *The Grand Illusion*. But there is a heroic quality in it that is understandable wherever men read or write or talk.

McCall's, December, 1938

THE CITADEL

ALTHOUGH it follows the career of a young doctor fighting his way from Wales to London, A. J. Cronin's novel, "The Citadel," is really two books. In the first section of the novel, Dr. Cronin simply and bitterly told the story of a young Scotch doctor who came with high intentions and great courage to a mean, poverty-stricken, backward Welsh mining region.

Even if you've never been to what the British blandly call "the distressed areas," you could see in these chapters of the novel the rows of dank, gloomy stone houses, the pale, stubborn wretched men, and the frightened, beaten women. With all the care of a first-class surgeon, Cronin gradually led his Scot into the alleys of ignorance and despair that had trapped the medical men of the community, and he created a fine character in Denny, the cynical alcoholic surgeon, who served as an interpreter of this doomed valley.

Except for the West Indies section of "Arrowsmith," I know of few more exciting chapters in modern fiction than the one in which Andrew and his world-weary friend blow up a sewer as a final desperate attempt to end a typhoid epidemic which is blithely ignored by a golf-playing public health officer.

As Dr. Cronin (more power to him) is a better doctor than he is novelist, he failed to create a full-blown, flesh-and-blood heroine for his young doctor. You believe he fell in love and married a school teacher, but most of the love scenes—if you can call them that—are pat and routine. What you do believe in really is the courage of the man who overcomes poverty, ignorance on the part of both the miners and his associates, and who fights through an investigation of silicosis-pneumonia against almost inhuman odds. This is the first novel.

The second attempts to show London society, and the mannerisms and chicaneries of Harley Street society doctors. You believe there is a Harley Street, and you know there are society doctors, but in the novel the characters are thin and wavering, and you cannot quite believe that the same Andrew Manson who battled ignorant coal miners could, with no more justification than a poverty he always has known, sell out his honor for an automobile and a street address.

Thus, when King Vidor took over the job of dramatizing "The Citadel," he had more problems than a director usually has when he attempts to translate a novel for the screen. He had one dramatic and clear-cut novel, the first section; he had a loose and at times unbelievable last section to straighten out; he had a heroic leading man, but a nebulous heroine.

More serious, however, he had a topic which might have made his employers uneasy: he had a doctor's novel that in no weasling manner excoriated the society doctors of London and their scandalous nursing homes. Dr. Cronin should be very pleased. Mr. Vidor and Robert Donat as Andrew make the first section of the picture as stark and bitter as a director and actor possibly could. You believe in the stubborn doctor—and I doubt if you ever will forget the opening scenes in the picture of those bleak, ghastly distressed areas.

With the help of as fine a collection of bit actors as I've ever seen on the screen, Vidor and Donat simply but quickly outline this first section, and until the young doctor goes to London, *The Citadel* is an example of great movie-making.

It is in the London sequences that the picture, as the novel, falls apart and loses its curt simplicity. Although Mr. Vidor, by adroit direction, and Mr. Donat, by first-class playing, make you feel that the young Scot is seduced into fee-splitting and into nursing rich old hypochondriacs by the ingenuity of his worldly Harley Street associates, it still is not quite a reasonable psychological transition.

The golf game and the scenes in the nursing home are amusing and brisk and beautifully played, but you cannot believe this is the same young doctor who amputated a miner's arm in a coal mine, who fought his superior in order to discover that tuberculosis was an occupational disease that deserved workmen's compensation.

And Andrew's wife, unfortunately, is no more real on the screen than she was in print. She is jolly and loyal and all that a wife should be—except she has not one word, not one scene, in which she is a real person. And even if she could have been brought to life, Miss Russell, although a fair actress, resembles a simple schoolma'am about as much as Garbo resembles Snow White.

I think it is a fair criticism of Cronin's heroine that the one heartbreaking scene in the picture is not between man and wife but between Andrew and his first friend, the embittered Denny. And when Denny turns drunkenly, but tragically, and says, "There are so many mean people in the world, it hurts you when your friend joins them," *The Citadel* does reach the nobility of its theme.

Mr. Vidor, Mr. Donat, and Ralph Richardson, one of the best actors in England, do pull Dr. Cronin's novel together in a tragic conclusion, which, besides being good drama, happens to be a plea for public health and medical care.

It is fine that Metro-Goldwyn-Mayer allowed a director to state such a theme at a time when the government and the medical profession and the scientists of this country are, for the first time, facing the fact that we do not have adequate medical care. Thus *The Citadel,* for all its wavering, becomes more than an expert, well-played picture: it becomes a simple tale with a grave and disturbing implication, a story of an honest doctor attempting to use his skill to relieve misery and to save lives. And, however controversial the theme, I think any doctor will agree that here is a medical picture with no *Men In White* hokum, no hysterical, incredible melodrama, but with an honest story, honestly told. And that's a rare movie.

McCall's, January, 1939

PYGMALION

PYGMALION is a model production in that no movie producer could fail to make a fortune and please the public at the same time if he only would follow the principles of production employed in making this one.

First, employ an honest and gifted writer—*one*—to write a show; do not change it; employ a director to make it; give him enough money to employ expert craftsmen and talented actors. Selah! You have a good movie.

It is a simple pattern, but I should imagine it took more than a simple man to cajole George Bernard Shaw into selling his play to a movie company. After that, I presume it was no trouble getting Anthony Asquith to direct it, or Leslie Howard and Wendy Hiller to play in it.

It took a very bright man to remember that Anthony Asquith years ago made the only interesting movies in England; it was a shrewd man who remembered that W. P. Lipscomb wrote the celebrated Laughton picture, *Henry the Eighth*; and there isn't a producer in Hollywood smart enough to employ a musician as gifted as Arthur Honegger to write a special musical score for a dramatic movie.

Given an unimaginative, run-of-the-mill production, the old

Shaw play would have been testy and childish, because we have had stronger meat in the theatre since the old master wrote his study in phonetics and psychology.

But *Pygmalion* is no re-created stage play. Mr. Asquith and his crew took Mr. Shaw's professor and his flower girl, and whirled them into a sharp, tuneful, adroit motion picture. The play turns on phonetics—on whether a master of vowel sounds can take a "draggle-tailed guttersnipe" and pass her off as a great lady by teaching her proper English. Very well. The movie is about phonetics. And without, probably, your knowing why it is such an agreeable picture, the director and editor knit a marvelous background score into a fast-cutting sequence of sound and action.

You still have Mr. Shaw's dialogue, and every now and then a real honest laugh pops out of the old play; you have a splendid performance by Wendy Hiller, who looks like Helen Wills—which is no handicap; and you have Mr. Howard in a tailor-made part. But mostly you have an exhibition of real movie-making—of a sound score woven in and out of tense scenes, creating mood and tempo and characterization. That may not mean much to you, but I know you will find it a warm, pleasant, and delightful motion picture; one that will leave you with that cheerful feeling of having seen a completely satisfactory piece of work. And that, gentle readers, is because from the head man to the cutter all the people concerned with *Pygmalion* knew what they were doing and obviously enjoyed doing it. Mr. Shaw has waited twenty-odd years to get into movies, but he could not have made a more auspicious debut.

McCall's, February, 1939

LOVE AFFAIR

I HAVE never known a time when there was more interest in the motion picture, but the producers seem to be floundering in their attempt to meet the general demand for a more vital form of entertainment.

The actors and the writers and the directors themselves are taking an active hand in trying to free the screen, and the exhibitors and the unions and the government are going around in a merry whirl. Even the press has begun to print more than the usual press-agent handouts, and, for the first time since the industry became a profitable advertiser, has begun to make some blunt observations about the quality of motion pictures.

But it is a sad fact that neither in that part of the mail that doesn't ask me to go fry my face in deep fat, nor in those news columns that aciduously demand more variety and timeliness on the screen, does anyone stop to discuss the most important failure of the current movie: so few of them are well made.

The neatest and most expert movie of the spring is a light comedy, *Love Affair*, and as it was produced as well as directed by Leo McCarey, and as it shows a skill away and above anything we have had in a long time, the directors may have gained quite a bit in their argument for more authority. If all of them can do as well, the studios should give them control over all production, and willingly.

As usual, most of the press, and the public, will assume that the charm and flavor of the production is due to a very gifted couple, Irene Dunne and Charles Boyer, and to a great actress, Madame Ouspenskaya. But for all the crisp dialogue of Donald Ogden Stewart and Delmer Daves, and for all the admitted talents of the cast, still the major credit for *Love Affair* goes to McCarey, because he brought off one of the most difficult things you can attempt with film: he created a mood, rather than a story; he kept it alive by expert interpolations; he provided comedy when he needed comedy, and poignancy when he needed substance in his airy story; and he did it with a minimum of effort.

Actually, he has very little to tell save that two people meet on a boat and fall in love. Unlike a hundred other directors, he didn't need half the Cunard Line with which to establish his theme; he used two people. He has a worldly Frenchman rather weary of the world, and he needed only a few scenes with Madame Ouspenskaya, by far the high points in the picture, to tell us this.

It was inevitable that the picture should lose some of its airy quality as it came to its predestined end, because you never feel the lovers would ever actually be thwarted. For that matter, there is no plot whatsoever to *Love Affair*, yet you not only like the people, you want to see more of them—from the man who stops in the snow on Christmas Eve and sadly announces he has to lug a tree a hundred blocks, to a cheery landlady who delivers a hilarious account of her rocky marital life.

McCall's, June, 1939

THE 400,000,000; CRISIS

AT THE risk of his life, Joris Ivens, a talented and courageous Dutchman, went into the Chinese war zone and photographed the ragged army defending itself from the Japanese.

Recognizing some of the difficulties he had—even getting the film in and out of the war zone—and realizing the little amount of money he was able to obtain for his production, I still feel that *The 400,000,000* should have been a better motion picture.

It has a narration written by Dudley Nichols and spoken by Fredric March, and a score by Hanns Eisler—all men of impeccable credentials. But the narration does not give us a clear idea of what is going on in the picture. It wanders from newsreel interpretation to symbolism to first person narration, and it is confusing. The music—and I can assure you I would lean over far enough to catch my ears in my heels for that rare thing, an original score in a movie—is so thin, poorly scored, and meaningless, in terms of the film it accompanies, that it is difficult to believe a man as good as Eisler wrote it.

I sat with an audience that had an unusual tension for a movie audience. Here was a movie about something, a story of a great and tragic war in our time, and the audience wanted to know more about it. But the scenes were long and not too well edited; the narration did not have a concise and straight design—

Yet here was a great cameraman, a fine scenario writer (donating his services, I imagine), and a first-class composer, all failing to create a moving and original piece of work for the obvious reason that no one man sat down and sweated to weave all the threads into a simple, clear, well-designed movie.

I have heard that Ivens had tremendous difficulties shooting his picture, but I do not think *The 400,000,000* was an unsatisfactory job because he failed to get into the thick of the war in the far reaches of China.

It failed to be effective because no one edited film that, good photography though it was, did not add to a story; or cut narration that, excellent though it was, meandered. And no one asked the composer to write music that would not only be original but that would work with, or in counterpoint to, a simple story.

Even though *Crisis*, too, was made by a good man, Herbert Kline, and although it deals with a tortured people, the Czechs, and although it was written by Vincent Sheean, and narrated by Leif Erickson—this film also is an ill contrived picture.

No one could be unmoved watching children trying on gas masks and listening to lectures on the dangers of gas burns. It is hard to remain calm viewing pictures of the invader marching into a peaceful country, and to see England's Prime Minister walking up to Der Fuehrer to sell his country down the river. But those emotions you bring with you to the theater.

The scenes of Czechoslovakia in *Crisis* are strung together with no eye for design. The music is pitiful. And the narration is an editorial attacking the Munich pact, albeit with some basic and well-written political background notes.

I should think both *The 400,000,000* and *Crisis* put together were made for what it cost for one week's shooting of *Love Affair*. And no one on the *Love Affair* set was in any particular personal danger while he worked. Yet neither factual film is as good as it should be, and the concerned movie-goer may reluctantly conclude that perhaps the light comedies are the best the screen has to offer after all. Not true. The movie, for certain, is a difficult medium, but Hollywood very seldom tries, and the handful of courageous independents don't work hard enough.

McCall's, June, 1939

MOVIES WITH BLINDERS

SINCE 1931, our movie companies have been slowly losing the complete domination of world markets they held for almost twenty years. To a very small degree, they lost business to local competitors, but even in England, Germany, and France—the only three countries that produce movies of any consequence— the customers prefer Gable, Garbo, Lombard and our other stars to their own.

In a free market, our films unquestionably would continue to dominate the world's movie theatres, but two things have shut Hollywood off more and more each year from international trade: tariff barriers, or quota laws, and political censorship.

When Japan moved into China eight years ago, it marked the beginning of the end of a surprisingly profitable market in the Far East; when Hitler came to power in Germany, it marked the beginning of the end of our domination in middle Europe; and now that the Rome-Berlin-Tokyo Axis is riding high, the Hollywood corporations find their outlets being limited to England and France, and the formerly disdained Latin American distributors.

During this decade of contraction, the producers were frightened not only of the politicos who controlled foreign trade channels, but of the leaders in their own country who were voted into office. Thus, MGM paid an enormous sum of money for Sinclair Lewis's book, "It Can't Happen Here," and employed Sidney Howard to dramatize it, and then put it on the shelf, presumably for fear of annoying the dictators abroad. The same company has owned for many years a very dramatic novel, "The Forty Days of Musa Dagh," and has not put it on the screen, again because of international relations (although I can never remember a time when it wasn't considered cricket to insult the Turks).

Some years ago, Paramount bought Humphrey Cobb's "Paths of Glory," which already had been dramatized by Sidney Howard and produced on the stage, but to date Paramount has failed to make it, presumably because it deals with some rather ugly things that happened when part of the French army mutinied during the

World War. Even before Mussolini had found a chum and belonged to an axis, Paramount itself censored the headlong flight of the Italian Army as recorded in A *Farewell to Arms* (an otherwise very fine picture) for fear of retaliation in an already shrinking market.

Of course, while I know of no overt incident, the fact that England remains our best foreign customer has operated as a hidden censorship factor, and has again made many subjects taboo in Hollywood. We have not, for example, ever seen a movie dealing with the Japanese expansion in China, although the newsreels, foreign correspondents, and Mrs. Theodore Roosevelt, Jr., have freely discussed the savagery of the open bombings of Shanghai and the villages in China. The fact that British capital launched Japan in 1931 on its drive into Manchuria has meant that the English distributors probably would not be allowed to accept a pro-Chinese melodrama.

The Spanish revolution brought up so many headaches that the corporations simply ignored that war; besides Germany and Italy and England, there was the Catholic question to consider. So, outside of the ambiguous and emasculated *Blockade*, we saw no mention on the screen of the fact that Germans and Italians were blasting away at Spanish women and children, or that refugees and volunteers from every country in the world were blasting back, although there wasn't a hamlet in the country unaware of the basic facts of the war.

Meantime, while the totalitarian states were expanding abroad and frightening the producers away from any dramatic material that dealt with foreign affairs, the richest group of manufacturers in the country, timid by nature, would not touch a manuscript that dealt with unemployment, relief, labor, agriculture, or politics, although the newspapers and magazines—liberal and conservative alike—have argued over these issues as though the type were dipped in blood.

Thus, frightened by political issues both at home and abroad, the movie companies have imposed a censorship on themselves. In one of the most troubled decades the world has known—troubles that make for extraordinary drama—we have been shown on the screen either the tense situation Does She Love Him or have been asked to consider the glories of our great West back in granddad's day. What makes this an even more cowardly and stupid record is the fact that our government has been insouciant about the movie industry, and has at no time even mildly suggested discretion in the selection of dramatic material that might occasion international yah-yahs from the controlled foreign press.

McCall's, July, 1939

CONFESSIONS OF A NAZI SPY

IF YOU needed to be convinced that we have a free screen, one look at *Confessions of a Nazi Spy* should convince you, because the Warner Brothers have declared war on Germany in this one. Although it is hysterical, vicious, ill-contrived, and peculiarly ambiguous, I do not object to the picture because it will be a notable one in many ways; a direct assault on the rulers of a foreign nation, a direct accusation of espionage in this country on the part of Germany, it at least is a political movie that pulls no punches. It is, however, wild-eyed in itself.

It is based on a series of articles written by a G-man who is not, I am told by officials, held in great repute by the Department of Justice, for whom he worked. It is further based on as fishy a trial as I ever read about—a trial that involved an army deserter who wrote to a German newspaper, "I want to be a spy," and who copied military information out of a book he found in the New York Public Library. From the petty and almost burlesque facts of the trial, the Warners claim that the Germans are, through the German-American Bunds, attempting to organize a Nazi group in this country that eventually hopes to seize control of the government.

I have no doubt that this is true. There also are some members of the Ku Klux Klan down South who want to drive all Negroes, Jews, and Catholics into the Atlantic Ocean. There are a great many old people in the West who want $200 every month, and who are perfectly assured they are going to get it. There are some members of the American Legion in industrial cities who believe that members of a labor union should be shot if they attempt to strike and picket a factory. There are some perfectly decent, kindly, and old wealthy men who openly and freely say that the President of the United States should be assassinated.

In short, we are in troublesome, bloodlusty days, and a hysterical movie that concentrates on the dunderheaded German attempt to enlist support in this country either will leave you amused, because it is a little like a beer-garden burlesque; sad, because it is a symptom of war fever; or it will scare the living daylights out of you, because such inflammatory material can quickly lead to the events we saw during the war—German professors fired from colleges, German music boycotted—material, in other words, that might lead us to assault, rob, and ridicule a race in our country, as Hitler right now is robbing, assaulting, and killing the Jews in Germany.

I wish the Warner Brothers had produced Malraux's *Days of Wrath*, or Erika Mann's *School for Barbarians*, or any of the fine literature that has come out of tortured Europe. I wish they had shown the real horror of decent, innocent people caught up in a military rule, an exposition that might have been a warning to any war-crazy citizen, instead of focusing their attention on a childish spy scare.

But whether it annoys you or frightens you, *Confessions of a Nazi Spy* is an important picture. From now on we should see some action on the screen; with this precedent there is no possible way any producer could argue against dramatizing any social or political theme on the grounds that he's afraid of domestic or foreign censorship. Everybody duck.

McCall's, July, 1939

THE DOCUMENTARY FILM

JUST TO write the words "documentary" and "factual" gives me a headache, because for the past four years I myself have been working with what have unfortunately come to be known generally as "documentary" films.

As in most fields in which education and social service are involved, there is more talk, analysis, and discussion of technique in a so-called documentary group than there is in four Hollywood studios; for every cameraman or director who knows the first principles of movie-making, your documentary group always includes twenty-five critics, fifteen philosophers, two poets, one man who knows a banker, and forty-five corresponding secretaries. Mostly the group meets; occasionally people actually do manage to turn out a motion picture.

In a country which, geographically alone, has never been filmed, it seems ridiculous that teachers in schools and colleges all want instructional film and cannot get it. With the thousands of feet of newsreels turned out every year, and with the proved audience interest in factual films, it seems nothing short of stupid that no producer yet has entered this field in a full and intelligent manner.

The answer, of course, is clear: there are no films because no one can see how to make a profit by showing them; there is no way to make a profit because there is no place to show the film.

Right now there are some indications that perhaps the factual film will develop. The Rockefeller Foundation has given a grant to the University of Minnesota and to several other organizations, with few or no strings attached, to make factual movies. But funds are not the only necessity. Training is very important. Hollywood is practically a closed corporation, and while it needs writers and new faces, I doubt that any young man could get a job as an apprentice in the sound department, the camera department, or the cutting rooms—three very important divisions of the industry—if he had no experience of any kind, and he can't get experience today if he can't get a job in Hollywood. Thus, it isn't enough to give a man a camera and some money and a recording table and say, "Make a movie." He must have trained people, and, at Holly-wood rates for sound and camera, even the Rockefeller Foundation might well wince.

The movie industry itself is the most backward of all our cor-porate industries. No money for experimental production is spent, and it puts aside little or nothing for research. Of all the producers, Walt Disney, who is experimenting with new ways of recording sound with Leopold Stokowski and the Philadelphia Symphony Orchestra, is the only one at the moment who is trying to make improvements in the mechanics of his business. Young directors, cameramen, and technicians have to come up the hard way: by working on feature pictures, by working in some other country, or by having the right relatives.

Hollywood doesn't know anything about the United States. From the old cathedral towns in the tip end of Illinois, to the Basque colonies in Washington and Oregon, to the Italians in the low, scrubby hills of West Virginia, to the French Canadians in Maine, you could route a factual crew of movie men for years recording the looks and the customs indigenous to this country and not be tiresome or repetitious.

But you would need money and trained men. If Hollywood con-tinues to neglect this field, it will be up to the schools, foundations, and the government to furnish equipment—and it's expensive. Perhaps by then the documentary or factual film will pay for itself. Or, of course, perhaps by then we'll have television and won't have to worry about movies at all.

McCall's, August, 1939

GOODBYE, MR. CHIPS

So far this season, the most overrated picture of the year has been *Goodbye, Mr. Chips,* and the most underrated *The Flying Irishman,* both being, as it happens, biographical sketches, one fic-tional, one factual.

I think the movie production of *Goodbye, Mr. Chips* hardly could have been improved upon; Robert Donat, Director Sam Wood, and the British studios have done as much with James Hilton's story as any production crew could have done. But the story itself has been so overrated since Alexander Woollcott discovered it and nursed it and the bewildered and modest author into international fame that I feel the story in this case is the most important part of the picture to be considered.

No man who writes a modest short story could be accused of delusions of grandeur, and it isn't James Hilton's fault that his little story was launched with overwhelming publicity. It just happened that he wrote what must be Mr. Woollcott's favorite short story for, apparently, Mr. Woollcott never has liked a play, an actor or an actress until the object of his affection was covered with mold, creaking at every joint, and long since measured for burying clothes. And it just happens that during the past two years, the theatre itself seems to have been turned over almost exclusively to necrophiles, in that death and the hereafter have been the themes of our most successful shows.

Anything is grist to the Hollywood mill, and I assume the producers made *Goodbye, Mr. Chips* because it was a best-selling story, because they have a good English studio, and because they must make so many pictures a year in England to meet a quota regulation—all sound reasoning on their part. It is fortunate for them, however, that a part of the theatre public has turned to melancholic reflection of past glories, and that they have come out with their picture in time to tap a current mood.

In "Our Town" and "On Borrowed Time," in "Shadow and Substance" and in both "Abe Lincoln in Illinois" and "The American Way," our playwrights have been pandering to a public that is tired of thinking about war and pestilence, and that is more than willing to have a good cry about the great old days, or the days to come hereafter.

A decade earlier, that same audience was enjoying "Broadway" and "The Racket" and "The Front Page," the mature plays of Eugene O'Neill, and the Marx Brothers, which in the days of raw gin and raw investment trusts, was good raw meat for the customers. (Ah, yes, those were the good old days, before Mr. Mencken and his professors passed slowly into mumbling old age.)

But while "Our Town" and "Abe Lincoln in Illinois" and "The American Way" seem to me hollow funeral pieces, lacking both the stuff of life and of drama, *Goodbye, Mr. Chips* is even more irksome. As in "Lost Horizon," Mr. Hilton wrote an unadulterated, escapist plea; in the one, he pleads that we should get away from all the harsh realities of life; in the other, he meditates on the glories of an oldster who lost the one pleasant thing in his life, and who has lived out a life of service in the grey, unworldly cloister of a boys' school.

It is tender, it is gentle, it is sentimental. It is, perhaps, charming. It is also moribund, it is funereal, it is death, which I consider neither charming, sentimental, nor tender, but inevitable and a damned nuisance.

McCall's, August, 1939

THE FLYING IRISHMAN

NO MAN ever has had a more accurate biographical sketch made of himself on film than Douglas Corrigan in *The Flying Irishman,* and I think a copy definitely should be stored in the National Archives in Washington.

Where *Juarez* and *Conquest* and *Union Pacific* and *Dodge City* are Sunday supplement, fictionalized, historical sketches, *The Flying Irishman* is an exact report of the life and times of an Irish boy from San Antonio who wanted to be a pilot, who barnstormed in an old crate trying to meet the requirements, who worked overtime, supported part of his motherless family, and who finally flew the Atlantic in order to impress the airlines, and who still, at this writing, isn't able to get a job as a pilot.

If there ever was an American hero, Douglas Corrigan is it. He naturally isn't popular with the public because he is both funny and sarcastic, as any aviation mechanic who had worked all his life trying to be a pilot would be; he has none of the ethereal tragic qualities of a Colonel Lindbergh, nor none of the barroom gusto of a John L. Sullivan. He happened to be a very determined, single-purposed boy, brought up in the social stratum occupied by a majority of Americans—the impoverished gentility.

By one of those accidents, the producers tried not only to tell that story with Corrigan playing himself, but to tell it with all the poverty and hard work that went into it; to tell that and to get across a fey Irish quality that marked their subject. Wondrously enough, they succeeded in doing what they set out to do.

By using a narrative technique, the producers told their story quickly and accurately; besides making an unusual picture, they have, for the first time, demonstrated a way to take the best of the quick news presentation of the newsreels and *The March of Time* and to use it, to the best advantage, in feature movies.

I think it is unfortunate that the public felt the picture was merely one of those personal presentations and stayed away from the houses where it was being shown, because it was tired of hearing about Corrigan and his mad exploit. Of all the pictures that have been called "historical" or "documentary" or "factual," here is one. Besides, it is hilariously funny, even though, as he indicated in the last line in the picture, the young Irishman still doesn't think it is funny that no one will let him be a pilot even after he flew the Atlantic in a plane fastened together with baling wire.

McCall's, August, 1939

Grand Illusion
Front Page   *The Citadel*

All Quiet on
the Western Front

A Nous la Liberté   Public Enemy

Anna Christie

Snow White and the Seven Dwarfs

Horsefeathers

The Private Life of Henry the Eighth

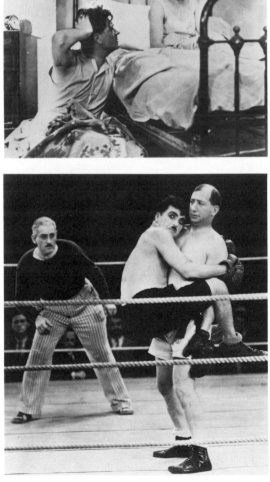

The Early Forties

I AM perfectly willing to admit—for the sake of argument—that I know nothing about men and women, but particularly about women; that, in fact, I've never seen a beautiful woman in my life.

And to continue the argument, maybe I've been wrong about Ethel Barrymore and Elsie Ferguson and Lynn Fontanne and Katherine Cornell and Gertrude Lawrence and Patricia Collinge and Ruth Gordon and Judith Anderson and Helen Hayes. But after a decade, I still cannot find Greta Garbo either attractive, exciting, amusing, or talented.

And I will take the scene from *Ninotchka* in which Miss Garbo is presumably reading a letter from her lover, and play it from here to South Africa and back, and if there is a man in the audience who can tell from this scene that Miss Garbo is about to relinquish the one love in her life and is not, as she has every appearance of doing, carrying a trayful of hot soup and trying not to sneeze—if that scene convinces any man he's watching a woman in love, then perhaps I might admit I'm wrong.

I read in the newspapers that Miss Garbo had changed her personality as well as her haircut in this picture; that, in fact, she

179

tripped through this production like Dorothy Gish flitting through D. W. Griffith's old daisy fields; that she chattered like a debutante at a football game, and went around the set laughing like a mad thing.

I must have seen the wrong picture. True, Miss Garbo does give voice to a modest laugh when Melvyn Douglas takes a tumble in a restaurant, and she does smile rather absent-mindedly at him when she meets him in Constantinople and decides to leave her job with the Soviet Government. Except for one titter I might have missed, this is the extent of the mad gaiety I saw in the picture.

McCall's, February, 1940

GONE WITH THE WIND

THERE are two stories to be written about *Gone With The Wind.* One of them is a simple account of the most incredible publicity campaign about anything we've known in a decade, and that includes Prohibition, elections, and wars.

The combination of the most driving, expensive, and ruthless producer in the movies, young David Selznick, and one of the richest young men in the country, Jock Whitney, and the most powerful studio in Hollywood, MGM, would be formidable enough to make a Townsend president. They had the most extraordinary best-seller of our time to work with, and they employed an old-time Hearst reporter with an incredible imagination, Russell Birdwell, gave him plenty of money, and turned him loose—and you had a three-year vaudeville show called *Gone With The Wind.*

Never in our time has a movie opening hit the front pages of metropolitan newspapers, and I cannot remember even in the crazy days of movies that a governor proclaimed a holiday over a motion picture.

After three years of publicity, I was pretty tired of hearing about *Gone With The Wind.* I was exhausted, as it happened, when I went to see the picture, and I went into the theatre with the dread knowledge that I was going to have to sit through almost four hours of continuous pictures. I was not interested in seeing what happened to the book on the screen, I was merely interested in my job, which is reporting on motion pictures. I can report that *Gone With The Wind* is the business.

Whether it is the greatest picture of all time, or whether it is a motion picture of any import, seems academic to me. It is a novel put on the screen, commas, semi-colons, paragraphs and chapters, lock, stock, and barrel. The leisurely style of literary sentences, the slow development of character, the long descriptive passages, everything that belongs to the novel has been transferred to the screen, regardless of the fact that a movie irrevocably moves at twenty-four frames a second and ninety feet a minute.

Whatever lack of profundity one finds on the screen, whatever dissatisfaction you may have with a war that may seem too far away from you, whatever lack of flesh and blood you find in Ashley Wilkes, must have been lacking in the novel itself, because if there's anything lacking on the screen it must be only the book jacket, and the author's original galley corrections.

It is hardly correct to say that Vivien Leigh is a discovery because Alexander Korda had her in *Fire Over England*, and she gave an outstanding performance in an MGM picture, *A Yank at Oxford*. The fact that she has been in movies before, however, does not detract from the keen judgment of Mr. Selznick in casting her as Scarlett O'Hara. Not belonging to the religious sect that worshiped the book, I was not interested in whether or not Miss Leigh was "like" Scarlett O'Hara. She is a beautiful, spirited, and extraordinarily talented actress. Had she been one whit less talented, she would have been swept off the screen by Olivia de Havilland, who gives a mature, charming, and flawless performance as Melanie Hamilton.

The only full-grown man in the picture, Rhett Butler, was well-played by Clark Gable, but either Selznick made his one mistake in the writing of this part, or it was poorly written in the novel. Whatever the error, Rhett Butler for the most part is a wise-cracking and unbelievable character until way along about the third hour, when he has married Scarlett and their child is born. During these scenes Gable is fine, and certainly any other actor would have been ruinous to the picture because it was a poorly-written part.

Butler is the one character that is not in the picture but outside it. All during the war scenes (which are, incidentally, the most spectacular shots ever made anywhere by any movie outfit), Rhett Butler saunters through the mob commenting on the war; you are watching the end of a civilization crumble, and you need no off-stage lecturer with a pointer to explain it to you. Not only is it gratuitous, but it makes Gable seem a fatuous fellow. Again, Gable has to point out the moral of the story in almost every scene he has with Scarlett O'Hara. "We are alike," he gaily bellows practically every time he grabs the beautiful young lady. By the time he has told her this six times you get the point.

A dozen writers, including the late Sidney Howard, are supposed to have worked on the script, but there is very little original writing in the movie. Mr. Selznick himself is supposed to have put most of the script together. Whoever, and however many men did the job, it is not stage or screen dialogue. The sentences are long and finished. They belong to the mood, the settings, and the characters in the story. This is the first time in the history of movies a director or producer has been able to slow down the ordinary tempo of movie-making to such a degree, yet because of the inhuman length of the picture, the dialogue sounds comfortable and in exactly the right tempo.

Director Victor Fleming must have gone crazy trying to direct such dialogue, but he and his designer, William Cameron Menzies, did it by simply creating a moving pageant. Sequence after sequence opens with a pastel drawing, setting a mood; Mr. Fleming leisurely peoples these pastel frames with his characters, and then as leisurely directs them in their lengthy dialogue scenes. Mr. Menzies held the picture together. His sets and his colors flow into each other so smoothly and logically, from daybreak to sunset, that they in themselves tell a story. The costumes and furniture thus keep the mood, which should be enough to drive novelists crazy. The colors are magnificent, and, for the first time, you have faces in color that are balanced and natural.

But enough. Mr. Selznick and Mr. Whitney have made a picture that has given movies enormous prestige. They probably have ruined the movie industry, in that the only way the Napoleons of the West Coast can surpass this one is to do what they did: spend money like generals, take three years, employ the best brains in the industry, and cast the best actors of two continents.

The picture is too long, and the final adventures of the Southern wench could have been abbreviated considerably. But it is a movie version of a novel, fantastic in scope, extraordinary in detail, played better than any movie I've ever seen, and more colossal, stupendous, gigantic, and terrific than any picture ever has been, without at any time seeming pretentious. If I go on any longer, I might as well go to work for MGM.

McCall's, March, 1940

THE GRAPES OF WRATH

IF YOU leave out the rather inconsequential drivel about "Who Is Going To Play Scarlett O'Hara?," there has been more controversy about John Steinbeck's novel, "The Grapes of Wrath," than about any other novel that ever was made into a motion picture.

Although the work was a best-seller, and although it was commended publicly by both Mrs. Roosevelt and the President, although it was unanimously called by the literary critics one of the great books of our time, newspapermen and the public alike voiced a wry left-handed criticism of Hollywood by asking for weeks: "Will Hollywood make it as it was written? Do they dare?" etc., etc.

Don't ask me how these things happen or what causes them— but Darryl Zanuck, who up to this time has shown about as much interest in social justice as a submarine commander, has produced *The Grapes of Wrath* with as much fidelity to the original spirit of the book as any producer possibly could have.

I cannot agree with the critics that this itself makes the picture the greatest movie of all time. The picture does not have the same simplicity, ease, and unity it might have had because of errors on the part of the adapter, the director, and the producer.

Nunnally Johnson, one of the wittiest lads in movies, remarked when he was assigned to write the scenario of *The Grapes of Wrath* that he felt as though he were carrying around the Holy Grail. Actually, that is exactly how he treated the novel.

Once he had filtered out the profanity, he put himself to translating the characters and the spirit of the book into a scenario, and he succeeded magnificently save in his opening sequences, where there was no direct action. Here Johnson needed a movie director. Here he needed to think in terms of skies and brown land and, most of all, wind. He needed only to have written "drought" and then left it to the director to re-create the feeling of those dusty plains tilting from Oklahoma clear up to Canada, with their miserable huts and busted windmills. In fact, he needed only to have gone to the panhandle of Oklahoma and Texas and western Kansas and the Dakotas and eastern Colorado and said: "Photograph this—here is where they came from."

As he did not, then Director John Ford (who, by virtue of going to Zion Park in Utah to photograph his outdoor sequences in *Stagecoach*, made a Western action picture into a thing of beauty) at least might have started his picture with the Great Plains instead of with scenes that, even though they were from the book, did not give you a feeling of the land. In fact, the scenes in which Granpa and Muley sob over handfuls of dirt and talk about the land are self-conscious, prosy, and maudlin.

If you have not read the book, these opening scenes may puzzle or even annoy you. But stick around. Once the Joad family starts for California, you will see a tough, brutal, uncompromising motion picture; you will gradually begin to feel the hackles rise on the back of your neck, and finally, when you ride into the Keene ranch and see the Joad family herded into dog kennels and treated worse than dogs, you will start tearing the legs off your chair. There is a peculiar newsreel quality to all the latter part of the picture.

Here is movie making. Director Ford chose his bit players with a great eye—his migrants, his children, and his deputies and his cops,

cops, cops. With their shiny uniforms and big open roadsters, they become obscene in the clear California sunshine.

They could have chosen a better actress for Ma Joad, and they might have kept in some of the scenes that made her one of our great literary heroines, such as the scene where she grabbed a jack handle and decided to lick Pa. They certainly could have chosen a better actor for Casy, the preacher who lost the spirit, and they might have made his death a thing of horror, instead of a lightning-like scene of sudden violence. But I offer these criticisms only against the statement that it is the greatest picture ever made in this country, and I feel such quibbling is fairly stupid.

Whatever else it may be, *The Grapes of Wrath* is the first picture made in Hollywood since 1929 that deals with a current social problem, that has faithfully kept the intent of an author who stirred the country, that has reproduced the bloody violence that has accompanied an economic upheaval—a violence that has been reported in the press from many parts of the country besides California but never on film—a picture that records the story of a tragic American migration into slavery. It is quite a movie.

I cannot help but nag at Gregg Toland and John Ford, because I think the former is far and away the best cameraman in Hollywood, and Ford is one of the half dozen real movie-makers in the industry. It may be that they were frightened of their subject and felt they must make it artistic, instead of realizing that more than any Western horse opera they ever made, here indeed was a simple story of simple people. But for all the beauty of his night effects and the difficult trick shots he made, Toland did not get the size of the Southwest, nor the feeling of the sky and land in his camera, and John Ford didn't make him do it.

Also, Ford was uncomfortable with his family in the early sequences; partly because he had a great deal of dialogue, and partly because he didn't know whether to portray them as comic characters, tragic people, or poor whites, or what. And, with the exception of his leading man, and John Qualen, he had a very mediocre troupe of players to work with.

He did, however, have in Henry Fonda an actor who gave him one of the finest performances I have ever seen; in fact, you may forget that Fonda is in the company—his performance is so tough, undeviating, and simple, you may think he is one of the extras, or one of the actual migrants.

There is a scene in the book that made me cry, and it is the best scene in the picture. Here the author, director, cast, and producer all re-created to the letter and the spirit the work of a great writer: the simple incident at the hot-dog stand where Pa Joad buys ten cents' worth of bread. There, in one simple, dignified sequence is the story of a great people.

If this picture had been any better, I wouldn't have had the words to discuss it.

McCall's, April, 1940

OF MICE AND MEN

IT IS completely unfair to compare the second Steinbeck picture, *Of Mice and Men*, with *The Grapes of Wrath*. There never was the sweep, the lyricism, the profundity, the size in *Of Mice and Men* as there was in Steinbeck's major opus. One was written originally almost in play form, and was intended for the theatre, where it won the Critics' Award for being the best theatrical production of its particular season.

As far as Mr. Steinbeck is concerned, here again an author and a director scrupulously tried to preserve the words and meaning of his work, and to faithfully reproduce it on the screen. It was a difficult problem for several reasons. The story originally was one without movement, written around a bunkhouse and a ranch.

Again, the movie medium is so graphic that it was practically impossible to portray a feeble-minded man in a straight manner. The Germans and the French have managed it, but in photographic terms, by symbolism and mood, rather than by dialogue. Thus, while the words and characters are the same on the screen as they were in the book and in the play, they are awkward simply because they belong where they were originally—in a book and in a play.

But, admitting all these things, I was bitterly disappointed in Lewis Milestone's interpretation of the play. Where he needed all the skill he has shown many times, where he needed understatement and finesse, and above all, simplicity, he has presented Lon Chaney, Jr., as Lennie, and let him perform as though he were a cowboy Lear; he overplayed every emotional scene until his bindle stiffs needed only mufflers and boots to step into any "Way Down East" company, and while he has some very interesting direction at times, he also fails to keep his situations clear and logical.

Burgess Meredith gives an honest enough performance, Betty Field is excellent, and Charles Bickford gives a realistic, easy performance. The photography is above average and Aaron Copland has written an unusual musical score.

McCall's, April, 1940

DR. EHRLICH'S THE MAGIC BULLET

THIS HAS been the most exciting winter of motion pictures we have had in ten years, and for the first time since I have been in New York, the motion picture theatres have presented more varied, imaginative, exciting and even deeper drama than has the stage.

While the so-called legitimate theatre is offering a dozen light comedies (and some of them very light indeed), a few musical comedies, a revival, and a cheapjack melodrama concerning a Nazi consul, the movie screens during one week were showing *Gone With The Wind*, *The Grapes of Wrath*, *Of Mice and Men*, *Pinocchio*, two distinguished French pictures—*The Baker's Wife* and *The Human Beast*—and *The Story of Dr. Ehrlich's Magic Bullet*.

From a movie-making standpoint the French pictures, as usual, are the best of the group. Unfortunately, they probably will have a limited distribution so I shall mention them only briefly.

Renoir, who made *The Human Beast,* which may be his last picture for years, because like a great many other Frenchmen he is at war, has again, in his dramatization of Zola's book, used the camera to create mood, to tell a savage yet sad story in musical rather than literary terms.

Pagnol, who used to own, manage, and eat and sleep in his own studio, also is at war, and his studio now probably belongs to the government. In *The Baker's Wife* he has another "typical" French farce—but, like Renoir, he has found a superb and uncanny group of actors and has told his story with adroit characterizations and intimate details, as Feyder did in *Carnival in Flanders.*

It may be years before we see any more French pictures so I hope you have a chance to see these two fine examples of movie-making from the most advanced group making pictures today.

The best home-made product of the month is *The Story of Dr. Ehrlich's Magic Bullet.* It is a simple, grave and charming portrait of the German Jewish scientist whose greatest achievement was the discovery of an arsenical specific for syphilis, compound 606.

I imagine because of the astonishing fact that it now is possible to openly discuss social diseases on the screen that you may have done the movie an injustice and thought of it as a clinical picture. Actually, the discovery, after six hundred and six experiments of the specific, takes up but a small part of the story; the picture, for the most part, gives you a faithful chronological development of Ehrlich's scientific life. Directed by a German, William Dieterle, there is in the settings and the costumes, in the atmosphere of the hospitals and in the Koch Institute, a real feeling of authenticity. Without laboring the point, Dieterle and his scenario writers have managed to recreate some of the pride and grandeur that marked those nineteenth century giants who made Germany a Mecca for medical and scientific men the world over.

Ordinarily, giving an actor a full length beard to wear is as reckless an act as giving a small boy a sawed-off shotgun to play with, and frequently it has taken a Barrymore or a Muni weeks to recover from the experiment. Oddly enough, Edward G. Robinson reacted in quite a different manner. As the stubborn, cigar-smoking bearded little man with a bad lung, Robinson avoids every one of his facile tricks. He does not gesture, or rant, or resort to his rasping voice, or freeze into a posture; on the contrary, he presents as simple and charming and honest a portrait as I've ever seen on the screen.

Ruth Gordon, one of the best actresses in the country, for her second time on the screen has to be the wife of a famous man, and while it helps to keep the picture simple and to the point, it is unfortunate for her that she has no chance to display her skill and, in fact, has nothing to do but be a patient, kind, loyal wife in the background. The associates of Ehrlich were superbly chosen, Montague Love and Albert Basserman being particularly well cast.

There is one scene in which Ehrlich is invited to a large dinner party at the home of a rich dowager, played by that great lady, Maria Ouspenskaya. During the soup course she casually asks: "And what are you working on now, Dr. Ehrlich?" "Syphilis," he replies quietly, whereupon the entire dinner party hits the ceiling.

That, I imagine, might have been your reaction when you heard about *The Story of Dr. Ehrlich's Magic Bullet*. Do not be misled. It is an engrossing, beautifully produced, and almost tender motion picture, with a magnificent characterization of a great scientist.

The one thing that irritated me is a completely personal matter. In several of the trade papers Warner Brothers has announced that the picture is based on an idea by Norman Burnside. As it happens, the Surgeon General of U.S. Public Health Service, Thomas Parran, almost single-handedly, and almost overnight, lifted the taboo against mentioning social diseases in the press and on the screen. Also, as it happens, chapter twelve in Paul de Kruif's "Microbe Hunters" deals with the life of Ehrlich and is entitled "The Magic Bullet." I think the Warners might at least have given some credit to either of these men.

However, there is only one way to look at a gift horse, and *The Story of Dr. Ehrlich's Magic Bullet*, Warners or no Warners, is a superb motion picture.

McCall's, May, 1940

GOOD ART, GOOD PROPAGANDA

D URING the past five years there has been a great deal of sound
and fury about the documentary film. There are movie classes
being taught in many colleges and universities; the Museum of
Modern Art Film Library has a study course in the documentary
film which it has sent all over the country. The Rockefeller Foundation has endowed several motion picture groups; it has an association of film library organizations; it has endowed a modern
composer to do research in combining music and film; it has established a complete sound department, and put up money for production at the University of Minnesota.

The Carnegie Foundation has produced one film, *The City*, and
has set up a course in general functional arts at Princeton; the Alfred P. Sloan, Jr., Foundation has produced two pictures and is
engaged in a large epic study of America; and the British have sent
over several flights of lecturers to explain to our dumb but patient
citizenry the meaning of the documentary film.

I myself produced three motion pictures for the United States
Government, which were promptly labeled "documentary," and I
also engaged Joris Ivens to direct a picture for the REA and Robert
Flaherty to direct a picture for the Department of Agriculture.

Strung out in this manner, like an old minstrel band in a small
town, the documentary film sounds fairly important. Personally, I
feel that if there ever was a movement, a school, a development, it
is practically stopped dead in its tracks.

Harvard, Columbia University, and the University of Chicago
have for years been fiddling with schoolroom movies, and there is
no question that in a very short time most of the grammar and
high schools in the country will be using both radio and motion
pictures to supplement textbooks.

Classrooms and college dormitories give me melancholia, and I
know nothing about theories of education, so I shall avoid any
discussion of "educational" movies. To me all educators who write
long essays about educational films forget that the people they are
talking about (i.e., their students) go right around the corner from

the classroom and look at Hollywood motion pictures; they also listen to Charlie McCarthy and Jack Benny on the radio along with, possibly, the Philharmonic and the Toscanini symphonic broadcasts.

I cannot believe, then, that even a ten-year-old boy willingly would sit through a bumbling, inept, dry amateur movie in a classroom when he's already become accustomed to the finesse, the speed, and the excitement of a *Pinocchio* or of a *Grapes of Wrath*. I also assume that the same boy has sense enough to know that *Union Pacific* has nothing to do with history, nor does *Virginia City* have anything to do with the Civil War. Even if he can't or won't read, the child probably knows by instinct that such productions are spurious either as art, entertainment, or fact.

Good art is good propaganda. And educators, politicians, and little group-thinkers can't produce good art, or they wouldn't be educators, politicians, or little group-thinkers.

In the past twenty years, we have had Robert Flaherty's *Nanook, Moana of the South Seas, Man of Aran, Elephant Boy,* and, with F. W. Murnau, *Tabu,* and to me, the greatest of these was *Tabu* because Murnau was the greatest artist.

Flaherty, a gentle, courageous, lyrical Irishman, undoubtedly started what is the documentary movement. Flaherty is a poetic explorer, who has been at the ends of practically all the continents of the world; he has worked with Esquimaux, Polynesians, Indians, and Irishmen, not because he wanted to start a school, but because he loved what he was doing.

Ten years ago a cameraman went into the Southern Highlands, picked up a college football player working in a sawmill, found a mountain girl, hired some seven-foot mountaineers, and made *Stark Love,* a startling and beautiful picture in its day. Ernest Schoedsack and a wild-eyed but gracious war-time pilot, Merian Cooper, borrowed some money and made a picture in India about elephants, called *Chang,* that was very successful. There are a few others: *The Wave,* by Paul Strand; *The Spanish Earth* and *400,-000,000,* by Joris Ivens; *Crisis,* and, the most recent, *Lights Out In Europe,* by Herbert Kline.

What I am concerned with in this critique is whether the documentary, non-fiction, non-profit, or—to coin a final awkward word —the un-Hollywood film, has any importance either to movie makers or to the general public.

Practically all these pictures have been critical successes but have meant very little to the general public simply because Hollywood has had a lock on all the screens in the country and Hollywood is not interested in documentary films. Now, for the first time in years, the theatre circuits are interested in independent pictures— partly because Hollywood can't afford to produce expensive pictures now that it has lost its world markets, partly because there is an anti-monopoly suit in progress against the producer-distributor corporations.

If there ever was a time when the non-fiction film had an open market, this is the year. Yet I feel that the fiction, rather than the non-fiction, picture will be the most important type of movie we will get from the independent, new movie-makers, and for two reasons.

The first is because of the groups interested in documentary films. Just as they have in the theatre, in literature, and in politics, the extreme left-wingers in movies have taken the attitude that because a movie is liberal it therefore is "good." There is no easy way to write a novel or an essay, or to produce a movie. Thus, while I am personally in favor of the Chinese winning their own country away from the Japanese and while I personally was horrified at the Nazi invasion of Poland, I do not feel that just because a man has made a picture dealing with these subjects he has made a "good" movie.

Again—good art is good propaganda. If a man in Kansas City, profoundly uninterested in European politics, paid money to see some of the pictures I mentioned, he probably was bored—and rightfully so, because he saw aimless direction, heard a meaningless score, and viewed some third-rate photography.

Motion picture-making is a craft. There are endless ways in which a man may combine imagery with personalities, landscapes, words, music, and sound, but the rules of dramatic logic hold just as true for a man who is making a picture about unemployment as they do for a man who is directing Garbo.

It, of course, is totally unfair to compare the work of a man who had no money, no huge studio, no chance to remake his work, with that of a man who has half-a-hundred brilliant technicians and all the millions he needs to help him. But that is not my point. The documentary filmmakers for the most part are more interested in theory than in practice; they are more interested in the subject matter than in the tools they are working with; and when they turn out an inept picture they scream "fascist" at anyone who doesn't consider they have turned out masterpieces.

Hollywood has for years closed its doors against new technical talent. For years it has not developed composers, cameramen, sound men, or directors, and for a long time it has been my hope that some financial group would establish an experimental motion picture organization, documentary or otherwise, so that younger men could learn a complex trade—could work with music and sound and photography in an effort to broaden the potentialities of the film medium.

The documentary film groups have schools of theory and groups within groups, and they are always having committee meetings. As I have written before, no committee can edit a magazine, or publish books, or produce plays or movies successfully. It has been tried many times. More than that, there is no such thing as a school of art. There are only men; some have talent and some haven't.

Thus for all the lectures, committee meetings, study courses, and esoteric jargon, I find no documentary movement going on in this country. On the contrary, there are some young men with talent who are willing to work for low salaries as long as they can make motion pictures about facts more important to the commonwealth than whether Irene Dunne will marry Randolph Scott. However, I don't think they or their work will be really important to the public, schoolchildren, or movie men unless they strive to have just as good photography, editing, and music as Hollywood.

Even under normal conditions, most of these groups would be left-footed to me because they argue that their cause justifies their work—their work must be considered important because their faith is the true faith.

My second reason for feeling that whatever documentary movement was under way has stopped dead is a simple one—that is, there is a war going on.

If there is a private, educational, or governmental group with sufficient power and money to produce pictures of our country in our time using the language and the music of the people, if there is any responsible organization not interested in interpreting this life in terms of war, I haven't encountered it. The documentary school will be in uniform by the time it gets out of the faculty meeting.

McCall's, July, 1940

THE GREAT McGINTY

COMING across an unsung production that is gay, fresh, well-made, and thoroughly satisfying is as startling and warming as it would be if you dropped into a dingy-looking restaurant and a bright and pretty waitress served you with an exceptionally well-cooked dinner.

All during the showing of *The Great McGinty* I expected the writer-director to fall into old movie clichés, but at each turn of the story he came up with an amusing or inventive scene, and finally, when there seemed no way he could end his picture except with a standard, implausible happy ending, he wound up with a logical, but novel and gay finale that gave the picture a final fillip —accurate, in exactly the right mood, unexpected, and really funny.

There is nothing in the story, or in the names of the cast, writer, or director, to give you a hint as to the high quality of this picture. I hope, then, that Paramount Pictures goes to some length to advertise the name of Preston Sturges, who wrote as a director and directed as a writer in his first one-man production; that they explain that Brian Donlevy and Akim Tamiroff never have given better performances in movies; that, while she is no Miss America,

Muriel Angelus is miraculously well cast as a pleasant, honest, attractive young matron; and that, above all, they do everything they can to announce that *The Great McGinty* is the most entertaining picture they have produced all year, and that the former playwright and scenario writer, Preston Sturges, has blossomed overnight into a director as adroit and inventive as any in the business.

The Great McGinty starts like a five-alarm fire and never slackens pace for one moment until its unexpected conclusion. It is a story of two engaging scoundrels—of a bum who votes thirty-seven times one election night, and of a political boss who brings him from the gutter, through an aldermanic post, into the mayoralty and finally into the governor's mansion, simply because the bum is fearless, and because the boss likes to fistfight with him. I have never seen two more engaging scoundrels on the screen, and neither man ever steps out of character. They are thieves, vultures, enemies of the commonwealth, but as such they are highly honest and very likable because they never pretend to be anything else—save just once.

This honesty of characterization would be in itself enough to recommend *The Great McGinty*, but there is a woman in the story, and here again the author-director throws away all standard plots and creates a situation that is part farce, part burlesque, and yet completely romantic and charming. Furthermore, the woman never dominates the story. It is a tale of two scoundrels; they enjoy life, they admit they are scoundrels, and they never lose a night's sleep over the fact.

As you leave the theatre, of course, you begin to question the outlandish tale the author has given you, but then suddenly you recall the current stories of a few of our state political machines and realize that Sturges, with no attempt at writing a "social consciousness" drama, probably in a bawdy, picaresque fashion has told a truer story of politics than we've ever had on the screen. And, finally, he has told it better than any director has told any tale in many months. Adroitly, he uses music, parades, and bands to advance his story; he throws away dialogue where he can use banners, or bits of speeches; and he does away with pedantic scenes that slow up practically all routine motion pictures.

He keeps to his two men. The city is shown by street parades; there is a mad night at election headquarters, and a brief scene in which a contractor is brought to his knees by McGinty—all lightning flashes that do away with any necessity of bringing in superfluous characters and dialogue.

In fact, he has done enough ingenious things in his first production to easily take rank with the Frenchmen who have sent us such inventive, amusing comedies this past year, and he certainly has established himself as one of the top-flight directors in Hollywood.

The Great McGinty is a honey.

McCall's, August, 1940

THE BISCUIT EATER; OUR TOWN

WHILE it has none of the finesse that *The Great McGinty* has, I should like to mention *The Biscuit Eater*. I should like to point out that for once a studio actually sent a camera crew on location. The story concerned two small boys and some bird dogs; the producer took two small boys, went to Georgia, and photographed the swamps, the meadows, and the dogs, and while it is a little picture, it, too, is unusual, refreshing and in its way completely honest.

I have for many years petitioned the producers to go into the country to make their location pictures. In fact, if the studios would continue to give us more pictures like *The Great McGinty* and *The Biscuit Eater*, and one I am coming to, *Our Town*, I should feel ten years younger, because here are pictures without stars and without star plots; here are pictures that depend on movie-making—on mood, and music, and expert editing, and not on a highly-advertised star appearing in a routine, standardized, tailor-made movie plot.

From a technical standpoint, *Our Town* was one of the most difficult productions ever given over to a director and his crew. A Pulitzer prize-winning play, written by the stylist, Thornton Wilder, it owed a great deal of its success to the fact that it was a novelty; there were no sets, and the story of a "typical" New England village was for the most part narrated by the town druggist, played on both stage and screen by Frank Craven.

Thus, with no sets at all, and a narrator, the director had to start with no visual background of any kind, and with practically no action in his story.

Technically, *Our Town* is a beautiful production. The photography and the sets are charming. Guy Kibbee as a small town editor, Thomas Mitchell as the country doctor, Beulah Bondi and Fay Bainter as their wives, and Frank Craven as the sharp-tongued druggist who comments on the life and times of the village in the manner of an Edgar Lee Masters—all are excellent.

I was depressed and annoyed by the play, and depressed and confused by the movie simply because I could not understand the intent of the author unless it was to enjoy an afternoon's stroll in a cemetery.

To be sure, the story centers around the pastoral love affair of the children of the editor and the doctor, and in the play the girl dies in childbirth, whereas in the picture she dies, visits her relatives in the cemetery and then comes back to life, but I can give you no clue as to either conclusion save the author's own words: "You must love life in order to have life; you must have life in order to love life."

McCall's, August, 1940

THE LONG VOYAGE HOME

IT WAS almost thirty years ago that the handsome, tight-faced little Irish sailor who used to hang around the back room of a Christopher Street bar wrote his first one-act play, "The Long Voyage Home." And it was in about the same year, 1912, that John Ford wandered into the desert wastes of Southern California to start work in Hollywood.

Eugene O'Neill, Southern California, the movies, and Mr. Ford

have come a long way since then, but they finally are well met—
Mr. Ford's production of *The Long Voyage Home* is such a magnificent motion picture that even a Nobel prize-winner should be
pleased, and gratified, and rather astonished at it. For here is not a
picturization, or re-creation, or copy of a playwright's work; *The
Long Voyage Home* is a classic example of a motion picture presentation of a dramatist's characters, moods, and fancies; of his
creative intent, expressed in adroit, expressive, and proper motion
picture terms.

As with every fine piece of work, there are no labored efforts, no
patent effects, in this production. In easy, simple fashion it tells a
story of seamen working their way across the oceans in the tramp
steamer Glencairn, of their dreams and ambitions and brawls in
the crowded world of the forecastle of the tramp.

It is very funny, and very sad, and occasionally exciting, and it is
unquestionably one of the greatest motion pictures of all time.

To begin with, Dudley Nichols has done an amazing bit of car-
pentry in combining four one-act plays into a well-balanced and
cohesive movie scenario. This was a difficult problem to begin with
because with one-act plays the danger would be that the scenario
might develop into a series of episodic incidents that would build
to no logical climax.

What he did was to choose the leading characters who run
through all the plays, and then deftly to lift out the key incidents
in each play and knit them together. He rearranged the order of
the plays in logical form so that, whereas "The Long Voyage
Home" was written in 1912, "Bound East for Cardiff" in 1914, and
"The Moon of the Caribbees" and "In the Zone" in 1917, the picture now opens with "The Moon of the Caribbees" and ends with
"The Long Voyage Home."

What dialogue there is in the picture has been taken almost directly from the plays, but, if anything, Mr. Nichols has improved
it in translation. His death scene between Yank and Driscoll,
which has the meaning, the flavor, the exact key of the entire play
"Bound East for Cardiff," is brief, concise, and yet almost word
for word as Mr. O'Neill wrote it; the absurd and astonishingly
up-to-date Fifth Column sequence in the last part of the picture

contains some of the best movie dialogue I've heard; yet it, too, is in the bitter, ironic, exact key of the play "In the Zone."

Almost any good rewrite man might have worked over these old plays with as much care and attention as Mr. Nichols has shown. What he has done beyond this is the sign of a skilled and experienced movie writer, in that he eliminated dialogue, and put all but the most essential words into movie action for the director to handle.

Thus, there is hardly any dialogue at all in the first reel of the picture, yet it is scene for scene "The Moon of the Caribbees"— bumboat, women, fight (and what a fight), stokers, sailors, music, moonlight, and all. He introduces and establishes the crew of the Glencairn, and their relationships with each other, and includes enough of the original dialogue between Smitty and the Donkeyman to give you a feeling that he has merely adapted the entire play *in toto*. It is only when you read the play that you realize he has made an adaptation in movie and not dialogue terms, and that the picture is almost completely silent save for the off-shore music, and the singing and playing of the sailors.

I do not wish to be so academic that the picture begins to sound like a difficult evening in the theatre, and it would be easier to point out that Dudley Nichols already has to his credit two simple, direct movie treatments, *The Lost Patrol* and *The Informer*, written in conjunction with the same director, John Ford; that furthermore, both of them are sailors, and that they hit upon a story about sailors, knocked it together, employed a crew of Irish actors, and made an old-fashioned silent picture that is an excellent movie.

But this business of writing for the movies is more a matter of not writing, and so few men in Hollywood understand it. If they are of any account at all, they naturally consider their dialogue the most important part of the picture, so they leave it to the director or the cutter to worry as to how to translate that dialogue into action, with the result that many of their lines get thrown away on the set or on the cutting-room floor. Not so with the script for *The Long Voyage Home*. Here the dialogue was written for, not against, a director, and all of the words sublimated to the camera.

Of course, this is a director's and a cameraman's picture, and I imagine Mr. Ford had quite a bit to do with Mr. Nichols in preparing the original scenario. However they worked, they produced among other things the best picture about the sea I have ever seen. There is a burial at sea; there are scenes that really look like a storm at sea, not, as in *Mutiny on the Bounty* or such epics, like the Great Deluge.

I hope for this reason that Mr. O'Neill sees the picture because, while he may not approve of the dialogue changes, certainly here is a picture that re-creates the simplicity, the childishness, the melancholia, and the bitterness that was latent in his first work.

While I have said it is a director's picture, his crew of Irishmen almost takes the picture away from Mr. Ford. Barry Fitzgerald as an absurd steward, Thomas Mitchell as Driscoll, the bully of the forecastle, John Qualen as the little Swede forever tooting on his flute, J. M. Kerrigan as an outlandish, ingratiating crimp, Wilfrid Lawson as the Skipper, John Wayne as Oley, Ian Hunter as Smitty —are all so good it practically is a matter of which one of them can get a crack at a close-up or bit of dialogue, as to which of them is stealing the picture at the moment. Mr. Qualen and Barry Fitzgerald have the edge.

Then there is the photography and the music. Gregg Toland has long been the best cameraman in Hollywood, but his work in *The Long Voyage Home* is really beautiful, and although practically all his scenes were difficult to shoot, they all are so well done none of them is arty or stagey.

In the original plays there is occasionally a fragment of "Blow the Man Down." That's all there is to the music in the picture, which was an inspiration on Mr. Ford's part. For the most part, Johnny Qualen toots away at the chantey in the forecastle; once in awhile the tune is taken up by an accordion; and where it is absolutely necessary there are a few chords of music to bridge you from one sequence to another. This monotonous repetition is probably the best musical idea any director has had in Hollywood in years; a heavy, pretentious score would have fought against the emotional intimacy of the men huddled together in the forecastle of the Glencairn.

I wish Mr. Ford had eliminated one shot of the Union Jack, and

I would like it if he cut two lines of the death scene between Driscoll and Yank. Whether he rushes to do this or not, I have no other choice than to recommend that he be given all of the Academy Awards for *The Long Voyage Home* this winter—Toland for photography, Nichols for dialogue, the entire cast for acting, and Mr. Ford for direction.

McCall's, December, 1940

THE GREAT DICTATOR

CHARLIE CHAPLIN has been The Little Man to the world for almost twenty-five years, and he is beloved by more people—red, yellow, white, and black—than any other character in theatrical history, save, possibly, Walt Disney's inorganic mouse.

Thus, it is to Chaplin's everlasting credit as a person, as well as an artist, that he chose to gamble doubly in making *The Great Dictator*—that he risked destroying the illusion of the little man with the baggy pants and the over-sized shoes by making him speak—and that he chose for his subject matter the far-from-amusing Adolf Hitler and his Nazi regime.

The picture itself is a simple one, but it is about as difficult to discuss as it would be to write a report on a one-man band, because besides playing the dual roles of a shell-shocked Jewish barber and of Adolf Hitler, Chaplin wrote his own dialogue, and directed not only his own two characters, but a troop of first-class actors as well.

Younger generations, who take movies for granted and who remember Chaplin only in *Modern Times*, may find the picture lacking in continuity and uneven in tempo, and those who expected a complete evening of comedy and nonsense may be startled and disturbed when Chaplin steps out of character in the closing scenes of his picture, and from the bottom of his heart pleads for humanity and peace.

But whatever your age or recollection, *The Great Dictator* will provide you with an evening with Charlie Chaplin, an evening with pantomime by the master, an evening with a caricaturist whose psychological interpretation of Hitler is at times more frightening than amusing—an evening of comedy, satire, burlesque, fantasy, and tragedy, such as no other actor in the world could present.

The first part of *The Great Dictator* is in the nature of a prologue, starting with the First World War, in which Chaplin, in an over-size German helmet, tangles with an anti-aircraft gun, a dud from Big Bertha, gets lost in a fog, and rides upside down in an airplane—all in such satisfactory manner that you are convinced you're watching a more elaborate *Shoulder Arms.*

But whether wittingly or because of the nature of the story, Chaplin becomes a more subdued, mature, and appealing Chaplin than he ever has been once he arrives in Berlin's ghetto.

A victim of amnesia, he returns to his barber shop unaware of Hitler or the changes that have taken place in the world, and I don't suppose there are more satisfying scenes in modern pictures than the ones in which, a free and independent little man, he challenges the storm troopers who raid his shop. In fact, had he so wished, Chaplin might have made a whole picture of this life in the ghetto. And Chaplin, the director, can be proud of the acting, writing, and photography in these scenes, although had he set up the camera as he did in the old days—with old-fashioned lighting and no camera direction—and merely photographed the scene in which he shaves a customer in time to Brahms' Fifth Hungarian Dance, it would still have been a memorable section of the picture.

Chaplin the writer also did first-class work in the ghetto sequences. His poor Jews are neither pathetic nor sentimental. They are amusing, genuinely sympathetic, but in character always. And, while Chaplin does speak occasionally in these scenes, he manages to make his barber quiet enough so that you are hardly aware that you have heard him speak for the first time.

Chaplin as Hitler is something else again. For the first time, Chaplin attempts not so much comedy or mimicry as caricature— a definite impersonation not only of the manners and trappings of a known character, but an interpretation of his ego as well. The result is that, while most of the scenes and situations are burlesque, Chaplin as Hitler for the most part stays in character, and occasionally, as in his dance routine, he is more terrifying than comical.

Of course, when Chaplin started to produce *The Great Dictator*, Hitler was merely funny to far too many people. And there are half a dozen scenes that undoubtedly would have been uproariously amusing only a year ago, when Chaplin made them—his antics with the court artists, his constant rages at Hermann, and his first meeting with Mussolini. They still are funny, but you do not laugh loudly now. You can only smile, and remember the city of London and wonder . . . However, this serious and ominous overtone in the Hitler sections of the picture is relieved partly by the fact that Billy Gilbert plays Goering as a beer-garden comic, and mostly by the fact that Jack Oakie looks and acts so much like Mussolini that at times you think he must have been clipped from a newsreel.

Paulette Goddard, who up to this time has been merely fetching to watch, comes closer to giving a dramatic performance, as a ghetto waif, than she ever has in her brief career. But to those who remember the old Chaplin pictures, it will be a little distracting to find her made up—shoes, loose stockings, dishevelled hair and all —exactly as Edna Purviance was in the silent productions.

As the little man, Chaplin's pants are not as baggy, his shoes are not as long, and he doesn't skid around corners as of old. But in his barber shop pantomime, in an act where he tried to avoid being chosen as an assassin, and in his set-tos with the storm troopers, he is still the master. As Hitler, on the other hand, he looks younger and tougher, and is indeed a new character.

As a writer, he produced a well-written manuscript that would be a credit to any expensive production. As a director he allowed some scenes to lag at times, but this might be due to the fact that he himself acts in such a fast comedy tempo that ordinary actors and conventional dialogue merely seem slow in comparison. His actors were brilliantly cast, with the late Maurice Moscovich, Henry Daniell, Jack Oakie, Reginald Gardiner, Paulette Goddard, and his old-time crew of comedians all giving performances as good as they ever have under any director.

As a producer, he displayed more daring than any of his fellow-producers in Hollywood ever have in these troublesome years. He not only gambled with a world institution—his silent little man with his bowler and his stick—but he based his whole story on a subject that is taboo in the industry: persecution of the Jews.

He probably would have had much better newspaper notices had he eliminated the six-minute curtain speech at the end of his picture, and he might have made more money by doing so, but it is not a war speech, nor a plea for a special cause or a race; it is a plea for humanity, and I do not feel that is out of order coming from an artist who spent his own money to make his own picture, in his own way. It is his belief—and it is worth hearing.

As a writer, Chaplin might have found a literary or humorous ending for *The Great Dictator*, but offhand I could not suggest a literary ending to a picture that deals with Hitler and Mussolini and persecution of little people.

I may have left the impression that *The Great Dictator* is graver than it is, when actually it is a magnificent caricature of a grave world, rather than a grave comedy. Whatever your own interpretations of the picture may be, I am sure of one thing: you will have spent an evening with a great artist.

McCall's, January, 1941

FANTASIA

To the consternation of professional music-tasters and to the mixed bewilderment and delight of his vast audience, Walt Disney has produced the first successful concert in motion picture form. Regardless of the eventual effect of *Fantasia* on professional music groups, this picture has broadened the field of movie-making more than any production since Griffith's *Birth of a Nation*.

In *Fantasia*, Disney has developed color to an almost unbelievable point of beauty and mobility; he has pioneered an entirely new form of feature presentation, opening the way for producers to utilize the vast literature available in the short subject field for variety, or concert pictures; he has developed an entirely new method of recording and projecting music, immeasurably broadening the potential use of music and pictures; above all, *Fantasia* itself is an audacious, stirring, austere, and entirely new kind of movie.

Musically, the concert consists of six familiar eighteenth- and nineteenth-century classical numbers, and one fairly modern composition, Stravinsky's "Rite of Spring," recorded by the Philadelphia Orchestra under the direction of Leopold Stokowski. The concert is presented in two parts, with Deems Taylor appearing on the screen before each number, explaining in easy, intimate terms either the meaning of the score, the intent of the composer, or some bit of program gossip connected with the selection.

As it is a concert, not all the selections in *Fantasia* come off successfully. The opening number, Bach's "Toccata and Fugue in D Minor," is, as Mr. Taylor remarks, music for music's sake, and Disney chose to dramatize it by simple architectural forms darting and swelling on the screen in time to the rigid mathematical development of the music. Either Disney's sound men, or Mr. Stokowski himself, underlined the music as though it had been recorded for the abstract designs on the screen; the fiddle section is harsh and metallic, as it is throughout the concert when used in full volume, so that neither as a presentation of the Fugue, nor as a Disney short, does this opening number compare with some of the other selections.

The second number consists of six parts of Tchaikovsky's, "Nutcracker Suite," and for the most part is delightful, although the first and last parts—the "Dance of the Sugar Plum Fairies," and the "Waltz of the Flowers"—are repetitious.

The third composition is old-fashioned Disney: Mickey Mouse as the unhappy apprentice who tries his hand at magic, done to Dukas's "The Sorcerer's Apprentice."

The fourth and last number in the first half of the concert is a dramatization of Stravinsky's "Rite of Spring," and it is by far the most daring, powerful, exciting, and successful section of *Fantasia*.

Either Mr. Taylor or Disney managed to make even the intermission amusing; before the concert resumes, Mr. Taylor launches into a speech about the sound track, which is displayed on the screen, preceding which the Philadelphia Orchestra jumps into a mild groove and indulges in a little jam session.

The first number in the second half of the concert, Beethoven's Sixth, or Pastorale, Symphony, is the only unsatisfactory part of the picture. I feel Beethoven is as much to blame as Disney, and rather than sharing with professional music-lovers a horror that Disney sullied the name of the great artist, I think he merely created a dull dramatization of a dull symphony.

And while I think everyone will enjoy the burlesque of that old chestnut, "The Dance of the Hours," that follows the Pastorale, even this is a little self-conscious and not nearly as funny as some of the Donald Duck or Mickey Mouse shorts that Disney has made in the past. He burlesques the ballet by having the hours danced by ostriches, elephants, hippopotami, and alligators, but they dance too well, and they are a little on the coy side. There is none of that wonderful violence and outlandish invention Disney created for the William Tell overture in *The Band Concert*, nor any of that savage burlesque of old operatic favorites he used to do with his big-chested hens in such shorts as *Mickey's Amateurs*.

The seventh number is a savage dramatization of Moussorgsky's "Night on Bald Mountain," which leads into a concluding Hollywood Bowl presentation of Schubert's "Ave Maria."

As Disney has used music and pictures better than anyone in the world for years, I assume he intended *Fantasia* to be a concert in which his pictures would be dramatized by great music, rather than a concert of fine music illustrated with pictures. Whatever his intent, his imagery and drawings dominate the concert from beginning to end. There is no way to explain the hundreds of beautiful designs, or to explain the invention he employs to dramatize sections of the music, except for "The Sorcerer's Apprentice," which is a familiar legend, and Stravinsky's "Rite of Spring." Here Disney's intent was clear; he blandly decided to use Stravinsky's ballet music to dramatize his conception of the creation and life of this planet from the beginning of life to the death of the dinosaurs.

In this number, Stravinsky, Stokowski, the Philadelphia Orchestra, Disney, his six hundred animators, his sound men, and the

Technicolor technicians rolled up their sleeves and, with the help of zoologists, museum directors, geologists, and anthropologists, turned out a geology lecture, a course in music appreciation, an animation of prehistoric life, a conception of a drought—a synchronized combination of color, action, and sound such as you've never imagined possible on the screen.

There is nothing comic, or slapstick, or even amusing in "Rite of Spring." There is an uncanny, frightening mood in this section —the music so surrounds and encloses you, the animals are so surely and accurately animated, you feel as though you are watching a weird, coloriferous newsreel taken by some visitor from Mars during the early days of this planet.

As you probably have gathered, I feel the first section of *Fantasia* is a great deal more successful than the second, with "The Sorcerer's Apprentice," "The Nutcracker Suite," and the "Rite of Spring" all being eminently satisfactory, whereas neither the Pastorale Symphony nor "The Dance of the Hours" is up to the high level set by these numbers.

As each section runs over an hour, it may be that you are exhausted by the time you get to "A Night on Bald Mountain"— not so much exhausted as completely overwhelmed by the combination of color, movement, and the music that swirls at you from all directions of the screen. However, I feel Disney should have had an old-fashioned low comedy selection in his second section, and I presume he felt that was what he was doing in "The Dance of the Hours." But either the high company of the Messrs. Taylor and Stokowski subdued him, or he felt low comedy out of place in such an austere presentation; whatever his reason, "The Dance of the Hours" isn't as earthy and violent as a number in this place in the concert should have been.

I advise you to disregard the howls from the music critics. *Fantasia* is a Disney and not a classical conception of a concert, and even though the music is broader and more powerful than any you've ever heard from the screen, it is the imagery, and not the scores, which you will follow during the show. Thus, you can dismiss the complaints of the little hierarchy of music men who try to make music a sacrosanct, mysterious, and obscure art. Disney has brought it out of the temple, put it in carpet slippers and an old sweater, and made it work to surround, and support, and synchronize a brilliantly-drawn series of animated color sketches. Yet it is not a cheap, or easy, evening in the theatre; it is one of the greatest the movies have ever presented.

McCall's, February, 1941

NIGHT TRAIN

DURING whatever hours he and his cast weren't ducking bombs, a British movie director named Reed has turned out a first-class melodrama called *Night Train*, which not only is a good movie, but is rather astonishing in that the entire attitude of the author and director toward the Nazis is one of good-natured ridicule.

The story itself follows the sound pattern of *The 39 Steps, The Man Who Knew Too Much*, and *The Lady Vanishes*, but it is expertly directed, well played, and entertaining from start to finish.

A fetching brunette, Margaret Lockwood, and her father are kidnapped in England and taken to Germany on a submarine because the father is a noted metallurgist. The British secret service operator, gaunt Rex Harrison, follows her, and proceeds to make love to her while masquerading as a German officer under the noses of the German Admiralty and the Gestapo, most of the action taking place on that fateful day when England and France declared war on Germany.

The picture frankly borrows from its predecessors to such an extent that the two silly-ass Englishmen who worried about the cricket match in *The Lady Vanishes* again are on a train worrying in their thick-headed manner, and they probably will become stock British movie characters for as long as there are English studios.

The director—and I have no idea where they found him these days—has kept his picture well-paced and simple, but the dialogue is amazing—it is witty in the best *Ashenden, The Secret Agent* manner, and its subtle burlesquing of the Nazis would be hilarious at any time, much less from a movie crew that was being bombed while it was at work. And if the RAF doesn't worry the Germans, the fact that Englishmen could make as humorous and good a picture as *Night Train* under the circumstances certainly should.

McCall's, March, 1941

SO ENDS OUR NIGHT

THERE are several remarkable things about *So Ends Our Night*, not the least of them being the work of some actors who in the past have given some highly odoriferous performances.

A dramatization of Erich Remarque's novel, "Flotsam," it has the sprawling organization that seems inevitable when you attempt to follow the episodic events of a historical novel. There are many repetitious and pedestrian sequences, but the picture is so well-played, and produced in such sobriety and good taste, it is on the whole a noteworthy production.

The producer exercised good literary judgment in not attempting to bring the Remarque novel up to date. Many people have died in war since this novel was written, but because such tragic events have taken place since the days of 1938 and 1939, *So Ends Our Night* takes on perspective, and once again we are reminded of the thousands of homeless, abandoned wretches that wander the earth today looking for refuge.

There is, in fact, very little war or brutality in this picture. There are two love stories, and while the director could not make a straight, neat picture in attempting to follow the episodes in the lives of his two couples, the aimlessness of the direction in part contributes to the atmosphere of the production.

Even though you do not know at times whether the characters are in Prague, Vienna or Paris, it hardly matters. You know eventually the police will arrive, and the abandoned refugees will be on their way again.

The story concerns itself mostly with a young Jewish couple, superbly played by a newcomer, Glenn Ford, and by the best actress in movies, Margaret Sullavan, and with a former German officer who has been run out of his country because of his political activity.

The scenes between the German officer and his wife are about as charming, affecting, and well-directed as any love scenes I can remember on the screen, but the fact that Fredric March plays the officer, and Frances Dee his wife make them even more astonishing. Miss Dee has been in and out of pictures for several years. Quite a while back she turned in a prize-winning job as a neurotic young society girl in a picture called *Blood Money*. A little older, and quite a bit more appealing, she is so fetching in her brief moments in this picture I feel sure she is assured of another and longer movie career. As for Mr. Frederic March, even though I think he padded his clothes and was unnecessarily rugged and military and all that, he gives a very honest and simple portrayal of Captain Steiner that more than any other single factor gives *So Ends Our Night* authenticity.

You cannot help writing a great deal of drama into any production these days that deals with events in Europe, and possibly a great part of the tragedy in this picture is imparted by the news dispatches and the radio reports that come to mind as you watch this picture. Allowing for this, the producers, writers, and Director Cromwell deserve a great deal of credit for their honesty, and for not attempting to exploit current events. There is no flag-waving in this picture. There is no war-mongering or deliberate attempt to wring every situation dry of its emotional content. They merely present a handful of simple, decent people, caught up in catastrophe, and sent wandering over the face of the earth. They point out no moral and they suggest no solution. They are so honest, in fact, that even Eric von Stroheim, as a Gestapo agent, somehow manages to be almost sympathetic.

For the rest, it is a handsome, expensive production, superbly photographed, with an excellent lyrical score by Louis Gruenberg.

McCall's, April, 1941

CITIZEN KANE

A FTER two years of announcements, rumor, gossip, threatened lawsuits, and general sound and fury, Orson Welles and his Mercury Theatre group finally have released their first motion picture, *Citizen Kane*. It is quite a movie.

As a producer and director, Welles has brought a fresh, and, for the most part, successful story-telling technique to the screen, using radio dialogue and music devices in dramatic motion picture fashion.

He has presented a complete Mercury Theatre cast that is unknown to the screen, which is a welcome relief, particularly as most of them are talented as well as refreshingly new actors.

His story, written by Herman J. Mankiewicz, a bitter-tongued Hollywood old-timer, and Mr. Welles himself, is a vivid, savage obituary of a great man, and is better written than any movie scenario we have had in recent years.

The picture was photographed by Gregg Toland, who produced some miraculous scenes that even outdo some of his work in *The Long Voyage Home*. It is a big, elaborate, carefully planned and executed production, of which Mr. Welles and his Mercury group should be proud.

Its chief fault lies in the fact that Mr. Welles is not a real actor, and that in the last section of *Citizen Kane* the entire production resolves itself around him. A director, editor, and producer, Mr. Welles as an actor works from the outside in; a master of lighting, make-up, and melodramatic tricks, he nevertheless lacks warmth and humanity, and his careful, enormous production in the closing scenes falls flat on its face.

Gambling on a device that in less skillful hands might have been lamentable, *Citizen Kane* is an obituary told in a series of flashbacks. It begins with a *March of Time* newsreel that briefly outlines the career of Charles Foster Kane, just dead. An editor is not satisfied with the information in the newsreel and assigns a young reporter to interview all the people who knew the great man intimately to get from them their stories of their real relationships

with him. The reporter calls on the shrewd old man who had been
business manager of Kane's newspaper empire; he visits a caustic
old drama critic who is philosophically dying in a great hospital,
and who had been the boyhood friend of the great man; he interviews the whisky-soaked blonde who had been his mistress and his
wife in his last days, and he interviews the servants who had attended him in his famous castle, Xanadu.

Thus, the picture is told in a series of flashbacks within flashbacks. You see Kane in his youth as he was known to some of his
associates, and through them follow his career to old age. The reporter continues his rounds, and once again you start with a young
Kane and work to his old age.

Gradually, the picture outlines four periods in the life of the
great man—his newspaper career and his life with his first wife, his
political career and its sudden finale, his life with his former mistress and his attempt to make her an opera star, and, finally, his
lonely, empty old age.

As the picture opens with the death of Kane and inevitably
works towards that same conclusion, the authors attempted to
avoid the inevitable anticlimax by making a mystery out of Kane's
last words, which they do not explain until the concluding scene
in the picture.

They probably would have succeeded had they not carried their
story-within-a-story technique too far. In the concluding scenes in
the picture you are completely familiar with all the characters in
the story; you know the life, the manners, and the full story of
Kane, and they need not have hesitated to kill him off in a hurry.

Unfortunately, there is no one left by the end but Mr. Welles,
and he and the picture become ponderous to the point of tedium
in these last scenes. Few actors could have held your interest in
these closing episodes, for that matter, because the authors go to
such lengths to prove that Charles Foster Kane was a cold-blooded,
hollow-hearted rich man that you are content long before the picture ends to see him put away. A cold, vain, and unsympathetic
character to start with, Mr. Welles did not bring enough warmth
and power to his great man to make you interested in his last days.
Once you see his friends, the dramatic critic, and his little blonde

singer leave him, you are ready for the funeral, and you would be willing to forego finding out his last words if they would just lay Mr. Kane away quickly and decently.

Perhaps you might have felt more sympathy for the newspaper and mining magnate had the authors shown him more at work; that is, had they shown him actively managing his great empire at any time in the picture, you might have felt some sympathy for the loneliness of the man when he lay dying.

However, the portrait they did sketch is told better than any team of authors and directors have ever told any biography on the screen. The device whereby in a few scenes you see Kane and his wife at breakfast, and understand in a few seconds the cold years of their married life; the heartbreaking scenes in which you see Kane trying to make a great opera star of his little blonde; the vicious episode of a picnic, over which you hear the music and voices of Kane's "friends" while he and his wife have a quarrel—all these scenes are handled in a quick radio dialogue style that should profoundly change movie-making from now on.

Hollywood has been oblivious of radio technique during these years of radio development. Welles now has shown them how to use dialogue in fast overlapping scenes, and he has not done it tentatively or amateurishly, but in a masterful fashion. His use of pseudo-newsreel clips, of brief conversational characterization, are new and effective.

And, unless he has them all under contract, he probably will lose half his Mercury Theatre group to the other movie companies overnight. Dorothy Comingore, as his little blonde friend, gives a difficult characterization in perfect perspective. She is lazy, a bit coarse, pleasant and amiable, frightened and timid, and withal charming. Joseph Cotten, as the dramatic critic who once believed in Kane, is a handsome, mature player, but Everett Sloane, as the little Jewish man who starts with a broken-down newspaper and sticks with the Kane empire to the end, is really superb.

I cannot point out without getting into too much technical terminology the incredible difficulties of make-up and lighting that went into making a picture in this manner. The fact that most of the characters had to go from youth to old age, and not in progression but in flashbacks; that all of them had to stay in character from youth to old age in the script as well as in make-up and in their playing, may give you some indication of the boldness of the conception of the picture. *Citizen Kane* is quite a movie.

McCall's, June, 1941

SERGEANT YORK

J ESSE LASKY and the Warner Brothers have produced the first war picture that has any relationship with the people and the places we know—a picturization of the life of the most publicized hero of the first World War, Sergeant York.

And one of the reasons it is successful is that it is more the story of a mountain man than it is a story of war; for all its crudeness, it is the first movie of a Southern highlander that has any authenticity whatsoever since *Stark Love* was produced some thirteen years ago.

Based on what was probably a hastily written best-seller in its day, "The Diary of Sergeant York," the four screenwriters—Abem Finkel, Harry Chandlee, Howard Koch and John Huston—hacked out a first-class outline of a Tennessee mountaineer that seems true in every detail, and, fortunately, Mr. Lasky got Gary Cooper to bring it to life. Not, as we've pointed out before, that Mr. Cooper is any Edwin Booth, but by remaining honest, and trying no tricks, he makes his Sergeant York a sincere, if slow-witted, woodsman.

Save for the youngster who plays York's child bride, one Joan Leslie, who is very fetching, and some of the minor character actors, including Joseph Sauer, and two children, Dickie Moore and June Lockhart, the cast performs like members of the East Maine road company of "Tobacco Road." From the make-up put on all the characters, to the phony mountain the boys built on the lot (because, presumably, Tennessee was too far away to reach by train), to the outlandish still picture of the old Waldorf Hotel, to the false eyebrows on Walter Brennan, to the miniature set of bottom land (used instead of a scene of a real valley), to the muddy French road obviously dug in the middle of California sand, to the battlefield that looks like a toy soldier set, to, finally, but most reprehensibly, the Ye Little Irish Theatre performance given by Margaret Wycherly as Sergeant York's mother, the entire production has an amateur appearance which seems even worse than it is because of the sincerity of the story itself.

Sometimes the mountain accents are as thick as sorghum molasses and at other times the hillbillies talk just like ordinary people. Mr. Hawks, the director, must have seen a Mamoulian production some time in his life because he held a revival meeting in which the Baptists shake their hands at the ceiling of the little church just like they do every time the Eastman School of Music puts on "Porgy and Bess."

It is an uneven production, and no one was comfortable with the locale. Yet it is a strong picture, and an honest one, and the gradual development of York—from a hellraising ridge-runner to a conscientious objector to a fighting fool—is well written and the role is played with integrity by Mr. Cooper.

And this is more than enough. It is exasperating that the same studio will go to endless pains to do a movie such as *All This and Heaven Too*, with every artistic device known to the trade, and then hurriedly toss out such an authentic story as *Sergeant York* done up in the old, familiar Hollywood trappings. Had they exercised the same care, and spent the same amount of money, their *Sergeant York* might well have been a lasting bit of Americana.

The picture is the story of one American in a European war; it tells the history of his people, where he came from, and why he fought. It is timely and important. What's more, I will wager that unlike the war pictures that have dealt with Frenchmen and Germans and Englishmen and Russians and Dutchmen and Belgians and all the unfortunates of the Old World, this one will have every chance of high success.

McCall's, September, 1941

McCall's, November, 1939

LOOKING BACK

FIFTY years ago this month, Edison looked in a hole in a box and saw some little figures going around, creating a sustained illusion of motion. That didn't mean much to me at the time, so I shall dismiss the experimental history of the motion picture, which would take us clear back to Leonardo da Vinci, and begin with Mr. Hunter's feed store, which is where movies started as far as I am concerned.

We lived in a small Methodist-college town, and an extraordinarily pure one, in that the county had been dry for years, card playing and dancing were forbidden, and cigarettes were not even for sale, much less smoked. There were no pool halls, checker parlors, or places of entertainment whatsoever save the opera house, where periodically we could see Al Fields or Vogel's Minstrels, a road company of "Are You a Mason?," "Officer 666," or "Mutt and Jeff."

The college and the church dominated the town, and both of them offered quite a bit of entertainment; in fact, there was better music brought to the college than the citizens of the town have heard for many years, and while the only lecturers I ever heard were humorists—Ralph Bingham, Jerome K. Jerome, and Strickland Gillilan—I imagine the lyceum presented some fairly intelligent platform men.

I do not remember the first movie I saw—although I saw it about six times—because I was overwhelmed by the volunteer band Mr. Hunter furnished to celebrate the occasion. It was even bigger than the group that usually played at the County Fair, and Mr. Colwell, who played a silver cornet when he felt like it and ran the best men's clothing store in town even when he didn't feel like it, gave me three packages of chewing gum, a seat in the front row, and that band got in the groove and practically blew the roof off that old store for three solid hours.

For the first few months, Mr. Hunter stood out front and greeted all his fellow townsmen as they came in, and shook hands with them when they came out, and Talbot's drug store stayed open late so the elders could discuss the new contraption that had won the town over.

I still have no recollection of *Broncho Billy*, because the town barber played the snare drum regularly, even when the band didn't turn out, and the pistol shots and coconut shells seemed more exciting than the film, which broke, flickered, and burned up so often we seldom saw a show all the way through. I do remember asking about a funny man who wore a mustache, and not finding out who he was until Mr. Griffith put his name in the titles of the picture, and I do remember John Bunny and Sydney Drew and Flora Finch.

It is strange, reading Hollywood gossip columns today, to recall that in a highly religious town no one ever dreamed of associating any evil with the motion picture. Whenever Mr. Hunter had an extra-special, three-reel Saturday night, my mother would sing a solo; sometimes it was the solo she intended to sing the next morning in church. The movie, during those first few years, was as much a part of the social life of the town as the church and the college.

The Harry K. Thaw trial changed that. We didn't get the picture until years after it was made, I am sure, else I wouldn't have seen it; I remember I was forbidden to go, but went anyway and heard a man describing a shooting, which wasn't anything startling in my community, and I remember he had a pointer and indicated on the screen the points of interest, such as where the corpse lay in Madison Square Garden, and where Miss Nesbit sat.

From then on, the movies went to hell for a time: Annette Kellerman dived off a rock in a one-piece bathing suit, and some of the elders in the town really blew up; I never remember, however, a word about censorship, or even a sermon against the movies until at least ten years after movies came to town.

I do remember one great evening in the theatre; perhaps the most dramatic I've ever spent in a movie. In the first place, the tickets cost a dollar apiece, and the fact that my father bought one for me was fairly dramatic; in the second place, we had an out-of-town orchestra—not a band—in the pit, augmented by the few first-class musicians we had. The score included arrangements of songs we'd always played, and the picture dealt with the bitter times we'd heard about, and it tore the town apart. I remember that night I sat longer than I ever had, and heard how his neighbors burned down my grandfather's mill and stole his furniture after he went to Lynchburg, and how Colonel Higginbotham took twelve kids and started out to meet Stonewall Jackson, and got shelled by a whole field artillery regiment, because McClellan, at the head of the valley, hysterically thought they were Jackson's vanguard. There was enough bitterness left that, for weeks after they'd seen *The Birth of a Nation*, families spoke sharply to one another.

It remains the one great movie ever made in this country; in size, in meaning, and in technique, no director has topped it in twenty-five years. Of course, we had only one Civil War, so perhaps it is only natural that we've had only one great movie dealing with it.

I do not remember those early movies well enough to even honestly list them in a record. I remember I saw *Dante's Inferno* and had the pants scared off me; it was a tremendous production for its day. I vaguely remember the other great Italian shows: *Quo Vadis* and *The Last Days of Pompeii*, but with nothing like the clarity that I can remember the wondrous gags in the Chaplin, the Keystone Kops, and the William Fox Sunshine comedies.

Except for comedies, movies bored me for many years; John Barrymore in *Dr. Jekyll and Mr. Hyde* and in *Raffles, the Amateur Cracksman* impressed me, but it wasn't until I saw the first full-length Chaplin pictures that I got excited all over again about movies. The memorable productions of those days were *The Thief of Bagdad* and the other Fairbanks pictures. *The Thief of Bagdad*, which is being done over again, was the first really beautiful movie ever made in Hollywood. It was designed by William Cameron Menzies, the director.

Someday some great scholar may be able to explain what was going on during the 1920s. We raised more wheat and cotton, and made more money, upset more apple carts, and wrote more plays and made better pictures than we ever had before or ever have since. Beginning with *The Gold Rush* right until the dread moment that Al Jolson said "hello Mammy" in *The Jazz Singer*, and in fact, for two more years, the French, Germans, and Americans had ideas, invention, courage; to this day, those men have never equalled the work they did during those brief years. They have had the advantages of wondrous gadgets, but they have done nothing with them to equal *Variety, The Crowd, Hallelujah, Sunrise, The Patriot, The End of St. Petersburg, The Gold Rush,* or *Tabu.*

I have written about it so many times for so many years that I do not wish to interpret the statement: *Sunrise* is the best motion picture made by anyone, anywhere, anytime. Actually, for pure form, *Tabu,* also made by Murnau, is a better picture; but it is a little movie in comparison with *Sunrise* (which was slightly marred by an ending Mr. Sheehan forced Murnau to put on the picture).

Mr. Colwell long since gave up his haberdashery shop on Main Street, and the chain stores line the once-shaded avenue that rocks to radio loudspeakers day and night. No road companies ever play the opera house, and the college can't get musicians to play concerts because you can hear Toscanini over the radio.

The youngsters go to the movies when they have nothing else to do, and bank night is the most exciting evening they have in the theatre. The broadcasting companies are going to begin televising regularly this winter, and they will televise movies more than anything else. Thus, after fifty years, it is time, not for a history, but for an obituary.

There never again can be the excitement over movies as there was in the early days because they went with automobiles, electricity, good roads, long distance telephones, and the general mechanical development of the age.

The people, as well as movies, have changed; they will demand heroes and heroines, however, and today they have turned to their radio entertainers; tomorrow it will be television, and perhaps we can develop a new flock of Murnaus to bring an excitement into the home approaching the fervor we had waiting for the film to start in the old feed store.

Citizen Kane   *Fantasia*

The Great McGinty
The Great Dictator   *The Long Voyage Home*

Gone With The Wind   *The Grapes of Wrath*

SOME BIOGRAPHICAL NOTES

Pare Lorentz can trace his ancestry on both sides of his family to the early days of colonial America. Several Lorentzes, who were Palatinates and Pietists, emigrated from Europe to the William Penn colony to escape religious persecution. His great-grandfather was among the earliest settlers in the wilderness of western Virginia, where the hamlet of Lorentz is named for him.

Pare Lorentz was born in Clarksburg, West Virginia, in 1905. His genes, he says, "were assembled by characters named Ruttencutter, MacTaggart, Boggess and Stalnaker." In 1909 the family moved to Buckhannon, a Methodist college town, where his father opened a job printing shop. His mother was a church singer, so young Lorentz was exposed to music early in life and studied the violin for many years.

Lorentz attended Wesleyan College and then West Virginia University. In 1925 he came to New York City and took a job as editor of a trade journal. Within a year he became film reviewer for Judge magazine, and later wrote film criticism for the New York Evening Journal, Vanity Fair, Town and Country, McCall's and King Features.

During the Depression, Lorentz became a producer of documentaries, capturing on film the drama and innovations of the Roosevelt years. Among his most notable films are *The Plow That Broke the Plains* (1936), which he wrote and directed for the United States Resettlement Administration, and *The River*, which won the world prize as the best documentary in the 1938 Venice Festival. When President Roosevelt established the United States Film Service in 1938, Lorentz was appointed director, largely because of the President's admiration for his documentaries. In 1940, Lorentz made *The Fight for Life*, winner of the National Board of Review's award for the best documentary of that year.

In World War II, Lorentz was a lieutenant colonel in the Air Transport Command and produced briefing films for flight crews in all theaters of war. He logged 2,750 hours of flying time (300 in combat areas), and received the Air Force Medal and the Legion of Merit. After the war, he was named chief of films, theater and music in the Civil Affairs Division of the War Department, and was responsible for these subjects in the occupied areas of Europe and Asia.

Tributes, official and otherwise, have been accorded him in considerable number by agencies of the U.S. Government, military commands, civic organizations and educational institutions. The University of Wisconsin at Oshkosh, which houses the Pare Lorentz Collection Room, made him an honorary Professor of Speech. He is a Doctor of Letters by virtue of an honorary degree from West Virginia Wesleyan College.

Lorentz has written several books, including one that he coauthored with Morris Ernst, "Censored—The Private Life of the Movies." He also wrote "The Roosevelt Year" and "The River."

Index